JOHN L. STODDARD'S LECTURES

PARIS   LA BELLE FRANCE

SPAIN

PLACE DU CHÂTELET AND THE SEINE.

John L. Stoddard's
LECTURES

VOLUME FIVE

CHICAGO & BOSTON
GEO. L. SHUMAN & CO.
MCMXXV

PARIS

THE ROUND POINT OF THE CHAMPS-ÉLYSÉES.

PARIS

ARIS is preëminently the City of Pleasure. It is the cradle of the freshest thought, the newest fashion, and the latest luxury. Within its limits there is little else than sunshine, gaiety, and life It is the paradise of pleasure-seekers. Each window is an exhibition of art; each square the centre of some carnival; at every step we seem to hear the exclamations of the votaries of joy. Triumphal arches here amaze us, columns appeal to us, statues attract us, theatres invite us, and art mu-
seums tempt us to behold their treasures, glowing upon canvas or crystallized in marble. Gardens and parks lure us within their shaded haunts, where music floats among the trees. The boulevards, with their swift currents of tumultuous life, sweeping in opposite directions or circling in brilliant eddies in each open square, confuse and dazzle us as we behold them; while, best of all, historical associations add sub-

LOUIS XVI.

stantial charms to these ephemeral delights. In the French metropolis, To-day has for a constant background Yesterday. Present and Past here move side by side like substance and

shadow.   Relics of conquering Romans, souvenirs of the
Crusades, tragic mementos of the Reign of Terror, the brilliant pageants and the shame of various dynasties,— all these
are mingled here with the most exquisite refinements of the
twentieth century; just as across the gay and fashionable
Place de la Concorde falls the grim shadow of the Egyptian
obelisk.   The fascination of Paris is at least as old as the days
of the Roman Emperor, Julian, who, fourteen hundred years

PALACE OF THE LUXEMBOURG.

ago, called it his "Dear Lutetia."   Still more enthusiastic-
ally, therefore, after all these centuries of progress, must we
also cry, "O Paris! Paris! No city in the world can equal thee!
Thou art the unrivaled Queen of beauty, luxury, and pleasure, outshining all competitors in splendor, and without doubt
the most attractive, polished, sparkling jewel that glitters in
the coronet of Mother Earth."

Whenever I have had with me in Paris a friend entirely
unacquainted with the city, I have always led him, at the

outset, to its unrivaled nucleus, the Place de la Concorde. This is, in my opinion, the most magnificent square in the world. Whichever way the tourist looks—north, south, east, or west—a brilliant boundary confronts him. The spacious area itself causes the unaccustomed visitor to catch his breath in admiration and delight. The first bewildering glance reveals in the centre the well-known obelisk of Luxor, flanked by two sparkling fountains and guarded by a cordon of colossal statues.

THE NUCLEUS OF PARIS.

On one side is the swiftly flowing Seine, spanned by a bridge five hundred feet in length; upon another lies the Garden of the Tuileries; a third side opens into the Champs-Élysées; while toward the north a handsome street discloses the majestic portal of the Madeleine. Over the smooth, firm pavement cabs come and go, like insects in the sun or swarms of fireflies in the dusk of evening. Forty artistic shafts in bronze hold up around this area at night their torches of illumination, and two colossal fountains here are probably unsurpassed in symmetry and beauty. At first thought, then, this splendid square, crossed and recrossed continually by joyous crowds, seems to have been appropriately named, "The Place of Peace." But a moment's reflection almost leads one to believe that the title was given ironically. For on the spot where falls to-day the shadow of the obelisk, rose formerly the hideous guillotine, whose glittering blade in swift succession descended on the necks of the ill-fated Louis XVI, beautiful Marie Antoinette, and thousands of the nobles of France. Here, too, the brutal mob assembled day after day to cheer and sing the "Ça ira," as head after head,—young, old, proud, beautiful, and famous,—rolled from the bloody scaffold to mingle in the common basket that awaited them.

PLACE DE LA CONCORDE.

Chateaubriand was therefore right when he exclaimed: "We may erect fountains here, but all the water in the world would not suffice to wash away the stains of the blood that has here been shed." Yet who can realize this now, as he walks or drives upon this square amid a tossing tide of riders and pedestrians? For fountains sparkle in the sun, and thousands laugh and jest where deeds were done which leave upon the history of the race a brand as ineffaceable as it was sanguinary.

PONT DE LA CONCORDE AND THE CHAMBER OF DEPUTIES.

Few, for example, think to-day of the scene enacted here on the morning of the 24th of January, 1793. In the centre of this Place of the Revolution, as it was then called, stood a lofty platform, above which towered the blood-red posts of the guillotine. Around this on all sides surged a sea of up-turned faces. At length the royal carriage entered the en-closure. When Louis XVI alighted from it, he was at once surrounded by the executioners. He himself quietly removed his coat and cravat, but when they advanced to bind his

hands, he cried: "No! no! I will not have my hands bound!" A struggle would have ensued had not his confessor intervened. "Sire," he said, "submit to this last outrage. It is one more point of similarity between yourself and Him who will soon reward you." At this, Louis stretched out his hands, saying, "Do what you will: I will drink the cup even to the dregs!" Then with a firm step he ascended the platform and prepared to address the popu-lace. The drums were beaten to

THE OBELISK AND EIFFEL TOWER.

drown his voice, but he was heard to exclaim: "I die inno-cent: I forgive the authors of my death: I pray that my blood may not fall on France, but may appease the wrath of God." These were his last words. One voice alone, that of the priest, replied: "*Fils de St. Louis, montez au ciel.*" The spring was touched; the glittering knife slid down the grooves; the soul of Louis XVI passed into eternity.

Eight statues of colossal size are seated round this square, each symbolizing one of the prominent cities of France. The crape-enshrouded flags and wreaths which render one of them almost invisible, remind one that the city it represents is Strasburg, the gem of Alsace, the loss of which the French so bitterly deplore. A distinguished professional gentleman of Paris once said to the writer: "Men talk of peace, but it is only the combination of three nations against us that keeps us from attempting to regain those provinces. If it were only Prussia against France, we should have tried it long ago. Depend upon it," he added, "if Napoleon I should rise from the grave and appear again in Paris, all Frenchmen— Republicans, Royalists, and Imperialists— would be at his feet."

It is a short walk along the Rue Royale from the Place de la Concorde to the Church of La Madeleine. "Are we in Athens or in Paris?" we ex-

THE CHURCH OF LA MADELEINE.

claim, as we behold it; for it may well be called the Parthenon of Western Europe. It is a beautiful reminder of those classic lines which had the Acropolis for a pedestal, Pentelic marble for material, and for a background the Athenian sky. Two thousand years have rolled away since Grecian architects and sculptors placed before the world those glorious models which have conquered time, but we have not improved upon them. Wherever they are reproduced, even with less attractive stone, less perfect statues, and less wonderful embellishment, they charm us still, as do no other buildings in the world. Truly,

"A thing of beauty is a joy forever."

I never pass before this structure, in a carriage or on foot, without bestowing an admiring glance upon its stately flight of steps, its long perspective of imposing columns, and the grand height of its majestic roof. So much does it recall the temples of antiquity, that it at first seems incongruous that this should be a Christian church. In fact, it has not always been a sanctuary. Before it was entirely completed, Napoleon I decreed that it should be a Temple of Glory, where, every year, on the anniversaries of the battles of Austerlitz and Jena, imposing ceremonies should take place and eulogies should be pronounced upon the heroes who had fallen on those memorable fields. But after the collapse of the First Empire at Waterloo, the original plan was again adopted, and La Madeleine is now a church where worship is regularly performed.

The Rue Royale is by no means the only interesting thoroughfare leading from the Place de la Concorde. Far superior to it in size and commercial importance is the famous Rue de Rivoli, which borders the entire Garden of the Tuileries. Few streets are better known to foreigners than this, and few have had a more eventful history. One of a thousand incidents connected with this avenue is that of the return of Louis XVI and Marie Antoinette, when they

THE INTERIOR OF LA MADELEINE.

were brought back to the Tuileries by the people as prisoners of the nation, after their foolish and disastrous attempt to flee from France and to obtain the aid of their fellow sovereigns in putting down the Revolution. It is hard to realize now that these very arches beheld that humiliating scene. It was on a summer day. The heat was dreadful. The royal carriage proceeded as slowly as a funeral car. An

THE ARCADES.

THE RUE DE RIVOLI.

enormous crowd of nearly three hundred thousand people produced a cloud of dust which made it difficult to breathe. Several times the Queen threw herself back in the carriage, crying out that she was suffocating. "See, gentlemen," she exclaimed to the hideous faces pressing around the vehicle, "look at my poor little children. We are choking." "Bah!" replied a voice, "that's nothing. We will soon choke you after another fashion!" Meantime all the men in the crowd kept their

V. — 1

V. — 2

THE RUE DE RIVOLI.

hats on,— a significant thing in France. It meant that royalty had forfeited respect.

In passing through the Place de la Concorde, Louis XVI had noticed that the statue of the King there had its eyes bandaged. "What does that signify?" he asked. "The blindness of the monarchy," was the reply.

At present, in these long arcades, sheltered alike from sun and rain, a ceaseless tide of tourists ebbs and flows before a mile of tempting shops and sumptuous hotels; and the arches echo to a babel of strange tongues, in which at times the English dominates all others, even French. One should be careful never to say anything private here in English; the very walls have ears. In more senses than one we appreciate here the wit of

THE TUILERIES.

the tourist who exclaimed: " In Paris, when I do not wish to be understood, I speak in French."

Adjoining the Rue de Rivoli for a considerable distance is the Garden of the Tuileries, that large and beautiful expanse where children play, foreigners stare, and Frenchmen promenade, and where, in summer, several times a week, delightful military music stirs the air. Yet, to one who saw this part of Paris twenty-five years ago, something is wanting which evokes a sentiment of sadness. The handsome and historic Palace of the Tuileries is gone—burned by the Communists in 1871. For several years the ruins of the noble edifice were not removed, but lay here, as an impressive object-lesson, reminding one how the Parisian vandals treated that magnificent château which, for three hundred years, had been the residence of kings and emperors. It used to be the fashion to remark that in no country except

France could such outrageous scenes of violence occur. This criticism was unjust. History proves that no one nation can monopolize the spirit of destruction. It is a characteristic of the lower strata of humanity everywhere, in moments of intense excitement, to burn and ruin public buildings, including even monuments of art. Nothing could be more senseless, or more sure to alienate the sympathies of the civilized world. Yet, under different names, in almost every land

NAPOLEON'S SON.

the tendency is much the same. Just as the Communists endeavored to destroy the grandest structures and the rarest

art treasures in Paris, so Anarchists in England, Spain, and Italy have tried to blow up bridges, theatres, and assembly halls; and even in this land of freedom, rioters (almost invariably of foreign birth) have already done

RUINS OF THE TUILERIES.

enough to teach us, if we would be wise, the only proper way of dealing with a mob; for as a rule, the party of disorder has no

more power than it is allowed to have. I suppose the modern
world has witnessed nothing more imposing than many of the
scenes enacted in the Tuileries. A brilliant, yet a melancholy
one, was that which followed Bonaparte's return from exile
in Elba, when he had traversed France without the firing
of a single gun, and had regained his empire without the

loss of a single
life, having sub-
dued all opposing
forces by the mere
magic of his glance
and words,—a
deed unparalleled
in history. It was

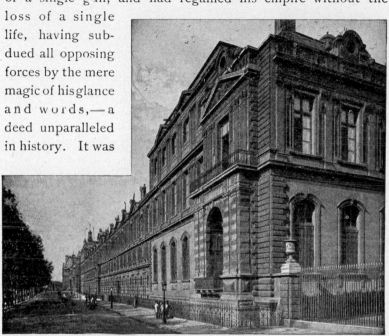

THE TUILERIES AND LOUVRE.

on the anniversary of the birth of his little boy that he had
thus reëntered Paris, but among all the faces grouped around
him here, one was still lacking to complete his happiness. It
was that of his child, the little King of Rome,—that little
prince who had himself been taken forcibly from the Tuileries, despite his tears and cries, as he insisted that his father
had told him to remain there; that child whom Bonaparte
had merely seen like a celestial apparition in his infancy,
and whom he was to see no more, save in delirious dreams

or visions of despair upon the wave-encircled rock of St. Helena.

Here, also, on the day of Bonaparte's coronation, the members of his family assembled in their gorgeous toilettes to join the imperial procession to Notre Dame where the

Pope himself was waiting to crown Napoleon Emperor of the French. Holding Josephine by the hand, Napoleon here received the congratulations of his brothers and sisters, who, at this supreme moment, seemed to forget the petty jealousies and hatreds which often make them seem so despicable in the light of history. Napoleon himself was evidently moved, but gave utterance to his thoughts in only a few laconic words: "Joseph," he exclaimed, turning to his elder brother, and gazing with pardonable pride upon the family group, "if our father could only see us now!"

THE GALLERY OF DIANA, TUILERIES.

The State dining-hall of the Tuileries, known as the Gallery of Diana, was particularly associated with the Second Empire of France, and was adorned with a marble bust of the Empress Eugénie, who presided over many banquets here with the grace and tact for which she was distinguished. Yet, in 1870, when the news of the surrender of her husband at Sedan reached Paris, she was obliged to flee in the disguise

of a servant from these historic halls, where she had reigned
as an empress for a score of years, and barely escaped the
excited populace without by taking refuge in the residence
of the American dentist, Dr. Evans, under whose protection
she was secretly conveyed to England.

At the end of this gallery, previous to its destruction,
stood a statue of Eugénie's son, the Prince Imperial, attended
by his favorite dog. There was something intensely pathetic
in the sight of that boyish figure. Few lives have seen a
dawn so full of splendor as had his, yet few have ended in
such speedy gloom. A strange fatality has seemed to follow
the offspring of the Bonapartes. Who that beheld Eugénie
in the period of
her glory, stand-
ing in the Gal-
lery of Diana
with her little
son, destined
apparently to as-
cend the throne
of France, could
ever have sup-
posed that she
would one day
make a pilgrim-
age to an uncivil-
ized continent,
and in the jun-
gles of Africa,

THE ARCH OF TRIUMPH, PLACE DU CARROUSEL.

—throneless and childless, a widow and an exile,—would
kneel down to bedew with tears the spot where her idolized
boy, born and reared in the Tuileries, had lain in death, his
body stabbed with sixteen spears, and even his eyes, which
had so often looked with love upon his mother's face, pierced

by the darts of naked savages! Beyond the site of this historic palace, one naturally steps into the spacious square
known as the Place du Carrousel, which was originally bounded
at one extremity by the Tuileries and at the other by the

A PAVILION OF THE LOUVRE.

Louvre. In the
centre of this area
stands an arch of
triumph, which, like
the grander one in
the Champs-Ély-
sées, was erected
by Napoleon I as a
memorial of his vic-
tories. Upon its
front of polished
marble, surrounded
by statues and re-
liefs commemorat-
ing heroes and heroic
deeds, is inscribed a
brief record of the wonderful campaigns of Ulm and Austerlitz, couched in those glowing words which Napoleon knew
so well how to employ to arouse the enthusiasm of his soldiers.
The bronze steeds now attached to the triumphal chariot are
not the ones that met Napoleon's gaze. The horses which
he placed here were brought, at his command, from Venice,
where they had stood for centuries above the portal of St.
Mark's Cathedral; but, after Waterloo, they were restored to
their old position in the City of the Adriatic.

Beyond this arch, and still forming the eastern boundary
of the Place du Carrousel, is the Palace of the Louvre. There
are some buildings in the world which do not seem the property of any one nation. They belong to mankind. They are
like cathedrals, continually open to all worshipers,—the rich,

the poor, the grand, and the obscure. One of these is the
Louvre,—the priceless art museum of France. It seems
needless to say, that the destruction of any one of its depart-
ments—Sculpture, Painting, or Antiquities—would be an
irreparable loss, not only to the present age, but to all coming
generations; yet it is well to remember that there are many,
even among the French people, who do not share these sentiments. Even as recently as the much vaunted nineteenth
century, Communists poured petroleum over this edifice and
undermined it, intending to destroy it with powder. It is
appalling to think that at that time a spark could have produced here an explosion which would have put the whole
world in mourning. As it was, the Louvre so narrowly
escaped destruction, that only by rare fortune do its works of

genius still re-
main to furnish
joy and inspir-
ation to the
world. "What
was the motive
of this act of
sacrilege?" one
naturally asks;
for in 1870 the
Louvre was not,
and had not
been for fully
two hundred
years, a resi-
dence of roy-

AMONG THE PICTURES OF THE LOUVRE.

alty. The cause was doubtless that sullen hatred felt by the
lawless and depraved for anything which seems to them symbolic of a class superior to themselves in culture and intelligence. An anarchist recently expressed this feeling at his

trial, when he cried "Let us destroy everything that is beautiful! Let us spit upon everything that enslaves us to a Fatherland! Long live anarchy!"

This sentiment is not a new one. Almost all the finest proofs of human genius since the dawn of history have been

MURILLO'S "IMMACULATE CONCEPTION," LOUVRE.

destroyed by man. It was man that shattered Egypt's grandest monoliths and temples; man that destroyed the Alexandrian library; man that set fire to "Diana's Miracle" at Ephesus; man that reduced to a pathetic ruin the matchless works of the Acropolis; and man that smashed to atoms, or left buried in the earth for centuries, the statues which we now exhume and worship as our models of the beautiful. Truly, one sometimes shudders at the record of his race!

One of the most magnificent apartments of the Louvre is the Gallery of Apollo. One could spend hours in this room alone. The ceiling is in itself a picture-gallery,—each painting

THE GALLERY OF APOLLO, LOUVRE.

placed there in a gilded frame. Upon the walls are life-size portraits wrought in Gobelin tapestry. In the glass cases are objects so precious that we should expect to see them guarded by a file of soldiers, instead of by the one attendant who is stationed here. For, separated from the visitor's fingers by only a thin screen of glass, we see the diamond-hilted sword of Bonaparte, valued at four hundred thousand dollars, the sword and spurs of Charlemagne, caskets and

gems which belonged to French queens, and even the famous Regent diamond, valued at three million dollars, and considered one of the finest in the world.

THE GALLERY OF APOLLO, LOUVRE.

A score of volumes might be written on the treasures of the Louvre which cannot be even mentioned here; but it is impossible to refrain from alluding to the most renowned and beautiful of all its relics of antiquity, — the Venus of Melos. One can perceive it from a distance; for the approach to it, as to the hallowed shrine of some divinity, is down a long avenue of sculpture. It seems incredible that as recently as 1820 this peerless figure lay buried in the earth on the small island of Melos in the Mediterranean. Shattered by some barbaric hand, it had been buried there for probably fourteen hundred years; but when discovered, it was

THE APPROACH TO THE VENUS OF MELOS.

immediately pur-
chased by the French
Government and
placed in triumph
here in an apartment
by itself.

The unfortunate
loss of the statue's
arms prevents a posi-
tive knowledge of
its original attitude.
Some artists think
that, when complete,
it represented Love
disarming Mars,—
the god of war,—so frequently associated with her in statuary.
In that case, the goddess was, perhaps, in the act of taking
from him his shield, one hand grasping its lower, the other
its upper border, while the chief burden rested on her knee.
Some, on the contrary, have supposed that she was holding
above her head
the apple which
the shepherd
Paris had given
her, as a token
of her preëmi-
nent beauty.
The second the-
ory fails, how-
ever, to account
for the promi-
nent position of
the left limb,
which favors the

RARE TREASURES.

idea that some object originally rested there. Probably the
question can only be satisfactorily determined by appealing
to the goddess herself, and as I gazed on her serene and
noble beauty, I felt inclined to murmur—

    O goddess of that Grecian isle
      Whose shores the blue Ægean laves,
    Whose cliffs repeat with answering smile
      Their features in its sun-kissed waves!

An exile from thy native place,
  We view thee in a northern clime;
Yet mark on thy majestic face
  A glory still undimmed by Time.

Through those calm lips, proud goddess,
    speak!
  Portray to us thy gorgeous fane,
Where Melian lovers thronged to seek
  Thine aid, Love's paradise to gain;

And where, as in the saffron east,
  Day's jeweled gates were open flung,
With stately pomp the attendant priest
  Drew back the veil before thee hung;

And when the daring kiss of morn,
  Empurpling, made thy charms more fair,
Sweet strains from unseen minstrels born
  Awoke from dreams the perfumed air.

Vouchsafe at last our minds to free
  From doubts pertaining to thy charms:
The meaning of thy bended knee,
  The secret of thy vanished arms.

VENUS OF MELOS.

    Wast thou in truth conjoined with Mars?
      Did thy fair hands his shield embrace,
      The surface of whose golden bars
    Grew lovely from thy mirrored face?

    Or was it some bright scroll of fame
      Thus poised on thy extended knee,
    Upon which thou didst trace the name
      Of that fierce god so dear to thee?

Whate'er thou hadst, no mere delight
　　Was thine the glittering prize to hold;
Not thine the form which met thy sight
　　Replying from the burnished gold.

Unmindful what thy hands retained,
　　Thy gaze is fixed beyond, above:
Some dearer object held unchained
　　The goddess of immortal love.

We mark the motion of thine eyes,
　　And smile; for, held'st thou shield or scroll,
A tender love-glance we surprise,
　　That tells the secret of thy soul.

IN THE LOUVRE.

　　In strolling down the Rue de Rivoli, one sees a singular statue representing Jeanne d'Arc, bearing triumphantly the standard of the Fatherland for which she nobly lived and bravely died. This statue is to me one of the most remarkable sights in Paris; not as a work of art, for it has many

faults, but on account of the sentiment connected with it.
Usually a wreath of flowers is lying at the horse's feet.
Sometimes there are no less than twenty there, each one
deposited with respect and reverence by deputations from
various provinces of France. They signify that Jeanne
d'Arc, by her absolute devotion, unselfishness, and martyrdom for France, is the personification of pure patriotism,
—*L'amour de la Patrie.** It is a
touching fact that, standing, as
France does to-day, well-nigh
alone in Europe as a great republic, she honors thus her mediæval heroine. From the material-
istic skepticism of the present
century this tender sentiment
springs like a lovely flower from
the asphalt of the pavement.
Heaven forbid that it should be
destroyed by ridicule! Mankind
has made its greatest progress, not
through the agency of its million-
aires, but by the unselfish devotion of its poor enthusiasts. Napoleon, that master of the art

STATUE OF JEANNE D'ARC.

of kindling enthusiasm, truly said: "Imagination rules the
world."

Not far from this statue of the national heroine of
France, stands the world-renowned Théâtre Français, frequently called the "House of Molière." To those who love
and appreciate dramatic art, the memories of this building
are inspiring. A score of years before the pilgrims landed
upon Plymouth Rock this theatre was in existence, and
was for some time managed by Molière himself. In 1768,
Voltaire's last play was here performed amid thunders of

---

* Jeanne d'Arc has now been canonized, and her statue is seen in many
churches in Paris.

STATUE OF MOLIERE.

applause,—the author himself, then seventy-four years of age, being present; and on this stage the indefatigable Molière, working till the last, was stricken with paralysis and died within an hour.

It is not difficult to understand how the Théâtre Français has acquired its brilliant reputation. Its company represents the very best that study and artistic training can produce in France. No care is omitted by its directors to foster genius and to give an opportunity for its display. Its humblest actors would be stars on any other stage, but here they are only members of a brilliant constellation. Even the part of a lackey is here rendered with consummate skiil. In order to become an actor in the Théâtre Français, one must have graduated from the French Conservatory, to which one is admitted only after a severe examination. Then a public trial must be undergone be-

THE THÉÂTRE FRANÇAIS.

PLACE DU CHÂTELET AND THE SEINE.

fore the most experienced of Parisian critics. Those who pass this
successfully may be accepted at the
" House of Molière," if there are
vacant places there; but usually
the candidates appear for a time
on the preparatory stage of
the Odéon. Moreover, this
theatre, which has a fund
reserved for pensions to be
paid to its retired actors,
is subsidized by the Gov-
crnment as a means of na-
tional education, and a certain number of the classic
dramas of Racine, Corneille,
and Molière must be per-
formed here every year.

RICHELIEU.

Directly behind the Théâtre Français, the tourist enters
that interesting portion of old Paris known as the Palais
Royal. When this magnificent palace was the home of the
all-powerful and wily Cardinal Richelieu it was naturally called

PALAIS ROYAL.

the Palais Car-
dinal; but, after
his death, hav-
ing become the
property of the
King, it received
the royal title
which it still
retains. Archi-
tecturally the
Palais Royal is
little changed.

Its arcades are the same, and two or three of its renowned cafés remain. But the glory of its shops, which forty years ago were unsurpassed for richness of display, has passed away, most of the leading jewelers having migrated thence to the boulevards or to the Rue de la Paix. This famous building, too, although associated with some of the most thrilling epochs in French history, was set on fire by the

APPEAL OF CAMILLE DESMOULINS.

Communists, and narrowly escaped destruction, together with the adjoining theatre of Molière. The world hardly appreciates how little of ancient and artistic Paris would have been left, had not the anarchists been thwarted in their horrible designs.

One hundred years ago this garden formed the favorite rendezvous for respectable citizens, who here discussed the affairs of state, much as the old Athenians did within their market-place; and here, one day in 1789, the tidings were proclaimed that Mirabeau's famous appeal to the King had

PLACE VENDÔME.

met with an insulting answer; that between Paris and Versailles were massed fifteen regiments of foreign mercenaries;
and, finally, that the very next day was the time appointed
for the people's delegates to be dispersed, arrested, or imprisoned, according to their notoriety; while any persons who
resisted   were to be mercilessly cut
down   with grape-shot. There
was a cry of indig-
nation when these
facts were stated;
and one young

THE WORK OF THE COMMUNISTS.

man, named Camille Desmoulins, his eyes gleaming with
rage and tears, sprang upon
a table in this garden, and
shouted: "To arms! To arms!
This very night the Swiss and
German troops are to march
hither to massacre us. We have but one recourse. It is to

THE VENDÔME COLUMN.

defend ourselves!" This was enough. With lightning speed
the cry passed through the surging crowd,— "To arms! To
arms!" A sign was needed to distinguish friends from foes.
Desmoulins plucked a green leaf from a tree and placed it in his
hat. This was the origin of the green cockade. Immediately

all the trees in the garden were stripped of their foliage. The words and act of Desmoulins had in a moment called into existence an army and a uniform.

In the very heart of Paris rises one of the most imposing monuments of Europe,—the Vendôme Column. Like so

THE BOURSE.

many other famous features of the French metropolis, it is a creation of the first Napoleon. For Bonaparte never thought a triumph complete till he had reared a monument to guard its memory; and this commemorates the victory of Austerlitz.

No one can pass this column without admiration and astonishment. The bronze of which it is composed was furnished by Austrian and Russian cannon captured in battle by the French; and its entire length from base to summit is covered with elaborate bronze figures in relief, forming a miniature army, with cannon, horses, and accoutrements, ascending

in a spiral path to the colossal statue of the Emperor above.
The figure on the summit has not always stood here. When,
after Waterloo, the Bourbons once more governed France,
they took Napoleon's statue down. It was the one which
represented him in the cocked hat and old gray coat, immor-
talized on many a field of victory; and Louis XVIII no
doubt believed Chateaubriand's words were true: " If that
gray coat and hat were placed upon a stick and planted anywhere upon the coast of France, it would cause all Europe
to run to arms from one end to the other." Not content,

BOULEVARD DES ITALIENS.

however, with the removal of that statue, the Bourbons put
in its place a monstrous fleur-de-lis. But this combination
of the emblem of the Bourbon family and a memorial of
Napoleon was so absurd, that Louis Philippe, yielding to the
desire of the people, not only crowned again this shaft of

triumph with the present figure of Napoleon (clad, less appropriately, in the garb of a Roman emperor), but even asked of England the return of the Emperor's body from St. Helena. This monument, too, was shamefully treated by the Communists, for they respected nothing. Religion, Art, and History meant nothing more to them than they do to the anarchists of to-day. Hence, animated by a sense-

A PARISIAN BOULEVARD.

less fury, they pulled over the entire column, — a thick bed of tan having been previously laid along the street to mitigate the shock of the concussion. Happily, however, the National troops arrived in time to prevent the destruction of the bronze reliefs, and both the column and the statue have been carefully restored.

So long as any of the soldiers who had served under Napoleon survived, they always came here on the Emperor's birthday and on the anniversaries of his great battles, and hung upon the railing of the column wreaths of flowers. Even now such scenes are not uncommon. The only wonder is that, in view of the enthusiasm still cherished for the first Napoleon, such demonstrations are not more frequent. One recollects here the pathetic words of Napoleon's son, who, though born heir to a colossal empire, died virtually a prisoner

in Austria. To a friend who was returning from Vienna to
Paris, he murmured: "Say to the Vendôme Column that I
die because I cannot behold it."

From this historic monument a few steps brings one to
the Boulevards. I mean, of course, *the* Boulevards; for
though there are many new ones in Paris, the distinctive
name refers to the old ramparts on the north, which were

A PARIS OMNIBUS.

long since transformed into a line of splendid thoroughfares,
beginning at the Madeleine and ending in the Place de la
Bastille. No photographic view can do them justice; but
every visitor to Paris knows that, as a specimen of metropolitan elegance and life, they are, in most respects, unequaled
in the world. Through them for many hours of the day and
night pours a continuous stream of restless life, between a
rare display of jewels, paintings, laces, silks, and countless
other fascinations, which justify the witty saying of Voltaire:
"*Le superflu,—chose si nécessaire!*"

Perhaps the first feature of these boulevards to impress the tourist is the width of their sidewalks. These are usually thirty or forty feet in breadth, and, when crowded on a Sunday afternoon, or about midnight at the closing of the theatres, the long perspective of pedestrians on them looks like an army marching ten abreast. Another striking characteristic is the throng of vehicles between their curbs. With the exception of a few omnibuses, these are all cabs or private carriages.* One stands upon the curbstone as one might linger on a river-bank, and watches the swift current sweep along until the brain grows weary with the effort to imagine whence and whither.

Who can forget the omnibuses on these boulevards, with the ascending stairway in the rear, leading to that perambulating post of observation which Victor Hugo liked so well

---

* The introduction into Paris of thousands of motor vehicles has changed the character, but not the volume, of the traffic.

PALAIS DE L'INDUSTRIE, CHAMPS-ÉLYSÉES.

that he would often spend there hours at a time? To an American the Parisian system of refusing admission to a public vehicle after the seats are filled is a surprise. How he misses, at first, the crowds that in his native country walk upon his feet, half-dislocate his knee-pans, or sit upon his lap! How lax his muscles become when no more forced to use his acrobatic skill in clinging to a strap when the New York conductor roars out : "Hold fast!" as the cable-car swings around "Dead Man's Curve." In Paris, when the seats are occupied, the little sign "*Complet*" inexorably keeps out all intruders. This leads sometimes to strange mistakes on the part of tourists, one of whom is said to have declared: " I have visited every place in Paris except Complet; but whenever I have seen

A NEWSPAPER STAND.

an omnibus bearing that name it would not stop for me."

The most remarkable feature of the Parisian boulevards is the life in their cafés. Sometimes for a considerable distance one can see nothing in the lower stories of the buildings but cafés,—all blazing with electric lights, blushing in gorgeous upholstery, and multiplied in glittering mirrors. Before them on the spacious sidewalks are numberless little tables, where, on a pleasant afternoon or evening, sit hundreds of well-dressed men and women, laughing, talking, partaking of refreshments, or (in a state of tranquil happiness which we Americans with nerves can hardly understand) observing the

crowd forever passing at their feet. The sight of such a
boulevard at night invariably suggests to me a theatre, the
audience of which is seated in a dazzling auditorium, watching the actors on a mighty stage.

AVENUE DE L'OPÉRA.

It is not strange that a Parisian, accustomed to the
beauty, luxury, and gaiety of his beloved capital, finds
absence from it an intolerable exile. Many years ago, in the
city of Hanover, Germany, I made the acquaintance of a poor
old Frenchman who had been living there for thirty years
without ever having been able to return to Paris. At last,
having inherited a little money, he went back to France. I
saw him subsequently in Paris, and he told me that his joy
had been so great in once more seeing these familiar scenes
that he had actually fallen ill from his excitement and delight.
He was then, in fact, just able to go out again, and I would
frequently meet him, walking slowly up and down the long

allées, in the Garden of the Tuileries, his hands clasped behind
him, a cane under his arm, and a look of supreme satisfaction
on his face. One day I found him seated at a little table in
front of one of the cafés on the Boulevard des Italiens. Pointing with one hand to the brilliant scene before him, and with
the other holding a copy of the *Figaro*, he joyfully exclaimed:
"Ah, monsieur, this is life! this is life! I am younger now
by twenty years than when I was in Germany." In truth,
there *is* something exhilarating in a great city. One may at
times grow weary of its restless energy, but its incessant
activity quite as frequently serves as a tonic. The heart beats

RUE AUBER AND THE GRAND OPERA HOUSE.

faster, the cheeks flush, the step is quicker, and one catches the
eager spirit, the earnest business tone, the sharp decision,
and the rapid interchange of thought so characteristic of
metropolitan existence. This partly accounts for the steady

migration from country to city which has marked the last half
century.   Men seek the intoxication of city life as they do
that of strong wine; and, having tasted of the stimulant, will
not leave the pavements for green fields.   After the roar of
the city the quiet of the
country seems to them
unbearable.   They love
the contact of their fel-
low-men, the wonderful
variety of sight and
sound, and the new at-
tractions that always seek
a city to gain a hearing
and a reputation.   The
heart of a great State is
like the heart of man,
which never rests; and
its streets and boulevards
resemble human veins

THE GRAND OPERA HOUSE, PARIS.

and arteries through which the warm life-current pulsates
ceaselessly.

An American in Paris soon perceives that the European
idea of streets and sidewalks is very different from his own.
With us they are thoroughfares, nothing more,—a means of
going from one point to another.   But in Europe, and particularly in Paris, they are places of recreation, where one meets
friends, partakes of light refreshments, and observes life.

Another peculiarity, not only of the boulevards, but of
almost all Parisian streets, is their gaily painted metal kiosques.
These are attractive even by day; but in the evening they are
especially picturesque, since they are lighted from within,
and with their multicolored panes of glass resemble mammoth
Chinese lanterns placed upon the ground.   In each of them
a woman's head emerges from a mass of newspapers, books,

and railway guides; for these kiosques are the news-stands of the city, at once convenient, useful, and artistic. In fact, one cannot speak too highly of the artistic forms in which commonplace objects in Parisian streets are cast. Theatrical programmes, for example, are displayed on pretty circular towers instead of monstrous bill-boards of unfinished wood, and even the lamp-posts are of ornamental bronze, each one a work, not merely of utility, but of beauty.

The streets themselves, like those of most European cities, are admirably paved, and on the corner of each one, however small, is seen its name in large, white letters on blue enamel. The buildings, too, instead of being painfully irregular, have a uniform height; and, best of all, the hideous telegraph-poles, which, in our avenues, often rise like gallows to destroy their beauty, are wholly wanting here, since, for appearance as well as for safe-ty, all wires in Paris are put underground. The most prom-inent point on the Grand Boulevards is the Place de l'Opéra, — em-bellished by the wonderful Academy of Music, which

THE FOYER OF THE GRAND OPERA HOUSE.

in its vast proportions and magnificent decorations is unsur-passed by any similar structure, not excepting even the splen-did Opera House and Theatre of Vienna.

The situation of this Parisian Temple of Music could not

be improved. It stands in the centre of Paris; and if the Boulevards may be compared to an outstretched necklace, the Place de l'Opéra is its medallion, of which the Opera House itself is the resplendent gem. The choice of this most valuable site for such a purpose is an admirable illustration of the way in which the municipal government of Paris looks to the permanent embellishment of the city rather than to the saving of a little money at the cost of symmetry and beauty. Thus, in the very heart of Paris, a large tract of territory was taken by eminent domain. Buildings were swept away, streets were completely changed, and finally the imposing Avenue de l'Opéra was cut through narrow streets and shops for nearly a mile, connecting thus the Louvre and the Academy of Music, and displaying the latter to the best possible advantage. Subsequently, of course, the land on each side of the avenue and in the vicinity of the Opera House increased enormously in value. We often practically hide our handsome edifices by giving them no perspective, wedging them in amid a multitude of other structures; or, through a false economy, we make the rear of public buildings of a cheaper material than their façades. Not so in Paris. The Opera House is surrounded by some of the finest of Parisian thoroughfares. No narrow alleys cluster in the rear, where "supers" make their exits and their entrances. No low saloons cling to its walls like barnacles. It stands alone, imposing and majestic, possessing its own private courtyard like the area of a castle. The color of the stone of which it is composed is not so clear and creamy as it was a score of years ago, but nothing can detract from the harmonious outlines of the edifice itself. The gilded harp which the colossal statue of Apollo holds at such a dizzy height, reflects the morning sun an hour before its radiance falls upon the stairway leading to the portals. On each side of the roof, gigantic forms in bronze cut their triumphant silhouettes against the

PLACE DE LA VICTOIRE AND STATUE OF LOUIS XIV.

sky.   The dome resembles an imperial coronet, below which is displayed the beautiful façade, adorned with fine Corinthian columns, marble busts of celebrated musicians, and groups of stat-   ues in relief.

But if the ex-   terior of this
Opera House   delights the visitor, what are   his feelings as he
steps across the   threshold and
looks upon its   famous staircase?
This might be   likened to the
Scala d'Oro in   the Doge's Pal-

STATUE OF THE REPUBLIC, PARIS.

ace, over whose surface none might pass save those whose names were written in the Golden Book of Venetian nobility. At all events, only the richest and most elegant costumes seem worthy to adorn this glittering expanse; for the broad steps are solid blocks of snow-white marble, the balustrades are made of onyx or of alabaster, while banisters of jasper rest on pedestals of malachite.

After ascending a few steps of this staircase, one reaches a platform where the path divides to the right and left, apparently at the command of two colossal caryatides in bronze. Between their ponderous forms one sees the entrance to the amphitheatre and parquet, and, looking higher, discovers numerous bronze balconies, as delicately wrought as perforated screens, and scores of monolithic columns of polished granite or jasper from Mont Blanc. When one has stood by one of these balconies at the close of an opera, and watched the brilliant throng descending amid a blaze of light, he has beheld a sight unequaled in the world.

It is safe to say that every one who leaves this building after a performance is thoroughly satisfied with all that he has seen and heard. It is true, one does not always find upon the stage stars of extraordinary brilliancy; but the French claim, with reason, that it is not meteors, but fixed constellations, that constitute a firmament. Therefore, the troupe of singers here is not like a flock of migratory birds, pausing for a few nights in a temporary resting-place, but is a well-trained, permanent organization, whose voices and peculiarities become so thoroughly adapted to each other that they at last, together with the orchestra, produce the impression of one grand, harmonious instrument of sound.

The most elaborately decorated apartment in this building is its foyer. Such corridors are far more used in European places of amusement than in America. The reason is obvious. In European theatres, although the intervals between

THE INAUGURATION OF THE GRAND OPERA HOUSE.

the acts are usually longer than our own, there is never any
music to relieve the tedium of waiting. Hence, almost as a
matter of necessity, spectators leave their seats and stroll
about until the warning stroke recalls them for another act.
This custom is often insufferably wearisome to a foreigner,
who finds himself in the gay multitude a perfect stranger,
experiencing all the miseries of a ball or grand reception,
with none of their redeeming
features.

The eastern terminus of
the Boulevards is the Place
de la Bastille. Here stood,
a century ago, that stronghold of tyranny and cruelty,
the anniversary of whose destruction by the people is
the great national festival of
France.

The Bastille was an enor-
mous edifice of stone, surrounded by a massive wall
one hundred feet in height,
fifteen feet thick at the top
and forty at the base. Above

THE COLUMN OF THE BASTILLE.

this rose in gloomy grandeur eight huge towers. The whole
was encircled by a moat one hundred and twenty feet in
width and twenty-five feet deep. For more than five hundred years this monument of tyranny had rested on the breast
of France, and it is not exaggeration to say that the instances
of horrible injustice known to have been perpetrated within
its walls (not to mention crimes which found no place upon
the page of history) would fill a volume. The dungeons of
the Bastille were slimy with the mould of ages, they swarmed
with vermin, and only a few rays of light stole in through

narrow clefts in the thick wall. No fresh air could find an entrance there, to purify cells foul with corruption. It seems incredible that this huge emblem of despotic power could have been taken by the people. The garrison had every advantage, for, through loop-holes in the wall, it fired directly on the masses that assailed it. On the other hand, the bullets

ON THE CHAMPS-ÉLYSÉES.

of the populace struck harmlessly against the solid masonry. In a short time, one hundred and eighty of the crowd were dead, while only one of the garrison was slain. Yet this massacre was not in vain. There were among the garrison French soldiers whose sympathies were in favor of the people. At sight, then, of this slaughter of their fellow-citizens, they summoned the Governor of the Bastille to surrender. This man, who knew that he was hated for his cruelty and avarice, saw that in either event his fate was sealed. His decision was therefore prompt and terrible. Seizing a lighted torch, he rushed into the powder-magazine. There, almost within his reach, was enough powder to blow the Bastille and its environs to atoms, and bury fifty thousand people in its ruins. A moment more and this terrific catastrophe might have occurred. But two soldiers threw themselves between him and the casks of powder, and drove him back with bayonets. At last, a pistol at his head, he signed a note of capitulation. The bridge was lowered. A living deluge of the populace rushed over it. The Bastille was taken, and its prisoners were set free.

But this was not enough. The horrible prison was to be destroyed. It must have been a soul-stirring spectacle,—that of the population of Paris tearing down this fortress, in which had been immured so many innocent victims. During a year's time it was covered, day after day, with men, women, and even children, toiling with inexpressible ardor and enthusiasm. And when at last it had really disappeared, then, on the site of dark and loathsome dungeons, this spacious square was opened evermore to the sweet light and breath of heaven, while many of the stones composing the Bastille itself were formed into a bridge spanning the Seine, and are thus daily trampled under foot by thousands of liberated Frenchmen. At present, too, the site of the Bastille is marked by a stately column crowned by a gilded figure of Liberty, holding in one hand a torch and in the other a broken chain.

The western boundary of the Place de la Concorde is no less attractive than those which have been mentioned. As the square itself is easily the first of city areas, so the promenade of the Champs-Élysées, which begins at this point, is the most imposing of all avenues. The long perspective of the Elysian Fields upon a Sunday, or a holiday, is the most perfect spectacle of the

A CAFÉ CHANTANT, CHAMPS-ÉLYSÉES.

kind that any city in the world can show. On this ascending plane, a mile and a half in length, one gazes then upon a moving host of horses, carriages, and riders, flanked on the

right and left by a still larger army of pedestrians, behind
whom are acres upon acres of delightful shade-trees, cafés,
walks, and open-air theatres.

During the daytime, most of the places of entertainment
here lie dormant, but when the enchantress, Night, waves
over them her sable wand, they spring into activity and
splendor.   Rows of electric lights not only flood them with
illumination, but spell out their names and programmes
in characters
of fire. In a
word, the Elys-
ian Fields of
Paris form a
vast network
of light and
music, within
whose glitter-
ing meshes hun-
dreds assemble
to enjoy a long
nocturnal fes-
tival. At the
summit of this
promenade rises
the crowning

THE ARCH OF TRIUMPH, CHAMPS-ÉLYSÉES.

object in its long perspective, the Arch of Triumph of the
Star.   The reason for its name is evident, when one considers
its position; for, from this as a centre, radiate like the points of
a star, no less than twelve grand avenues, each one of which
is so spacious and majestic as not to lose much by comparison with the Champs-Élysées.   It was a stroke of genius to
place this Arch of Triumph here.   Its situation at the union
of twelve stately avenues, each of which sweeps away as
grandly as the radiance of a search-light on the sky at night,

THE ROUND POINT OF THE CHAMPS-ÉLYSÉES.

is unsurpassed, and makes the approach to Paris from this side the most imposing in the world. The Place de la Concorde at one extremity,
—the Gate of Triumph at the other, and the Champs-Élysées between them,—these form a trio that defies comparison. To say that this is the grandest triumphal arch ever constructed is a strong statement; but it is literally true. One is obliged to use superlatives in Paris. Built in the style of the old Roman arches, it nevertheless surpasses them

THE NAPOLEON GROUP ON THE ARCH OF TRIUMPH.

in its proportions and in the superb effect that it produces. As is well known, it was erected in memory of Napoleon's victories; in fact, its corner-stone was laid upon the anniversary of the Emperor's birthday. Around the summit, one hundred and sixty feet above the pavement, is a series of medallions, each of which bears the name of some important

v.—5

ON THE WAY TO THE BOIS.

battle-field; and on the sides are numerous marble tableaux in relief, portraying notable events in Bonaparte's campaigns. On each of the pilasters is a colossal group of statuary, the most remarkable of which portrays France calling on her chil-

dren to take arms in her defense. Another represents Napoleon crowned by Victory. Beside him kneels a suppliant figure, symbolic of a vanquished nation; behind him His-

tory records his exploits on her tablets; while over him triumphant Fame proclaims them to the world. Yet the revolving wheel of fortune, turned by the hand of Time, brings strange reversals and revenges. Thus, in 1814,

IN THE BOIS DE BOULOGNE.

under this then unfinished gate advanced the allied armies to celebrate, in the Place de la Concorde, the downfall of the first Napoleon; and, in 1871, the soldiers of Prussia came as far as this arch, to emphasize their triumph over France by the invasion of her capital.

Standing beside this noble gate on a pleasant summer afternoon, and watching countless carriages roll westward from the city, one naturally asks himself: "Where are these people going in such numbers?" It is easily explained. Their destination is the Bois de Boulogne, the charming park so dear to all Parisian hearts. If one knows Paris customs well, he can encounter in the Bois almost all the distinguished people of the French metropolis. For every one comes here. The only question is, just when to find them. Strangely enough, the morning hours are the ones when the most aristocratic ladies of Paris take their drives and walks in the Bois. Foreign pleasure-seekers usually make their appearance in the afternoon; but between ten and twelve in the forenoon these avenues are comparatively deserted, save by equestrian officers, ladies of rank, or gentlemen of leisure. It is a pretty feature of the Bois, that, though so fashionable and crowded in certain parts, a few steps from the thoroughfares will bring one into rustic scenes, where one is apparently a hundred miles removed from the great capital. It is in such places that I have often watched the happy family life which is so characteristic of the French.

It is a great mistake to base one's opinion of domestic life

SKATING IN THE BOIS.

IN THE BOIS.

in France on novels of ·a certain character.   One of the most
beautiful sights in France is the filial respect, reverence, and
love shown by a son or daughter.   In no country in the
world are parents and children seen more frequently enjoying
life together, in many instances deriving pleasure from simple things which we regard as valueless,—just as French
cooks will make a most delicious meal from food that we
would discard.

Upon a little island in the centre of the Seine stands the
historic church of Notre Dame.   The situation of this cathedral marks the cradle of the present city.   Two thousand years
ago, both sides of the river were lined with forests, and on
this island were the primitive dwellings of the warlike tribe
which was vanquished with difficulty by Cæsar in his conquest
of Gaul.   The name of these brave warriors, the "Parisii," is
still repeated daily in the words "Paris" and "Parisian;" yet
Frenchmen need not blush at such a derivation, for the
Parisii displayed the utmost courage in their conflict with the
Romans, and the testimony of their conqueror is that not a
Gaul abandoned his post, but that all of them were surrounded and slain, together with their aged chief.

The Cross of Christ has replaced both the altar of those barbarians and the temple built here by the Romans. For more than seven hundred years prayers have ascended from this shrine to God. What memories are awakened, therefore, by the sight of these square towers! What scenes they have looked down upon during these eventful centuries! To recapitulate them all would practically be to give the history of France. For example, above the pointed doorways, filled with sculptured forms, stands a long line of statues representing old French kings. The figures themselves, however, are not ancient; for, at the time of the Revolution the originals were broken in pieces by the mob.

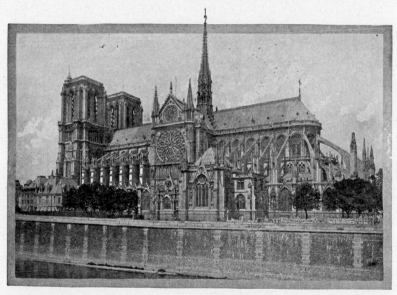

NOTRE DAME DE PARIS.

That was a gloomy period in the history of Notre Dame. Not only were the statues of her kings destroyed: Religion, too, was banished from this ancient fane. It was converted into a Temple of Rationalism, and in the ceremony of its dedication for this purpose, a woman of doubtful character impersonated here the Goddess of Reason.   One recollects with gratitude whose hand it was that opened this, and countless other churches, once more for religious worship; whose voice it was that summoned from French dungeons faithful priests, who, far too conscientious to abjure their faith, had languished there for years; and, finally, whose mind it was that recognized the need of a religion for the

INTERIOR OF NOTRE DAME.

nation, and re-established it throughout the empire.   It was the hand, the voice, and the mind of the first Napoleon.   This old cathedral is a noble speci-men of Gothic architecture. The long-drawn aisles, the fluted columns, the delicately pointed arches, the lofty intersections of the nave and transepts, the splendid windows of stained glass, through which the sunlight falls, apparently with the ruby and golden tints of autumnal leaves,—all these appeal to us with a mysterious charm that makes us speak in softer tones.   And yet, it is not so much the architecture that thus moves us as it is the memory of all that has occurred here during seven centuries,— the baptisms, the marriages, the burial services, the splendid pageantry of royal weddings and of coronations, the voices which have echoed here, the men and women who have trod this pavement, and whom these very columns have seen come and go like insects fluttering for a moment on the incense-laden air.

The tourist will be well repaid if he ascends the towers of Notre Dame to gain a comprehensive view of Paris. Directly beneath him he discerns the Seine, which here shoots onward like an arrow under bow-shaped bridges, dividing palaces and gardens in its flight. Outlined distinctly against the sky, although two miles distant, is that famous feature of the French metropolis, —the Eiffel Tower. " The path of progress," it is said, " is always strewn with discarded fears and falsified predictions." The success of the Eiffel Tower illustrates this statement. The proposal to erect it met at first with violent opposition. Hundreds united to protest against it in the name of art, declaring that it would be a blemish to the city. The effect of the structure is, however, quite the contrary. It is colossal, but not inartistic. Its splendid arches are prodigious, and yet beautiful. It is a miracle of strength and lightness; the loftiest structure

THE EIFFEL TOWER.

ever reared by man, yet graceful and symmetrical from base to summit.   Not only did it form the chief attraction of the Paris Exposition, but it still remains a permanent object of embellishment, visited in summer every day by hundreds, who are conveyed in elevators to its different stories.

It is astonishing to learn that forty draughtsmen worked for two years on the fifteen thousand different sections of this

tower, each of which required a separate design, exact to the one hundredth part of an inch.   In one hour, two thousand, three hundred persons can be lifted by the elevators to the first and second galleries and seven hundred and fifty to the top.   Upon the

THE BASE OF THE EIFFEL TOWER.

steps, and in its corridors, restaurants, shops, and theatre, ten thousand people can assemble at one time.   When crowded, therefore, the Eiffel Tower is like a vertical city,—a metropolis in a tube, a thousand feet in length, and letters posted there by its aërial citizens descend and go forth to the world by all the daily mails.

Looking down from the Eiffel Tower, one sees, not far away, a building which, in architectural design, has few superiors in Paris,—the Palace of the Trocadéro.   Although designed as one of the features of the Exposition in 1878, it still forms one of the permanent attractions of the city.   How

THE TROCADÉRO FROM THE SEINE.

well French artists understand the art of utilizing perspective!
The gradual approach to this imposing structure is rendered
beautiful by a most skillful and harmonious grouping of flowers, lawns, and fountains; and when, on festal nights, like
that of the 14th of July,—the anniversary of the taking of
the Bastille,—the palace and cascades are all illumined, the

THE TROCADÉRO.

effect can never be forgotten. The name, Trocadéro, is
derived from a Spanish fort at Cadiz, captured by the French
in 1823. There is, however, nothing Spanish in the architecture of the edifice. It savors rather of the Orient. Its lofty
towers, each two hundred and seventy feet in height, recall
the minarets of Cairo, and, with its curving galleries to the
right and left, it has the form of a colossal crescent. Although
called a "palace," the Trocadéro is, strictly speaking, a
palace only of the arts and sciences. In the main body of

PALACE OF VERSAILLES.

the building is a concert-hall seating six thousand persons, and in its curving wings are some of those artistic and historical collections which have now become so numerous in Paris that, if united, they would fill to overflowing another museum like the Louvre.

Versailles is almost as much a part of Paris as the Champs-Élysées. At all events, no one would think of leaving the French capital without paying a visit to the place where Louis XIV and his successors lived in splendor until the crash and chaos of the Revolution. The town of Versailles is, in

A VIEW AT VERSAILLES.

itself, dull and unpretentious; but its magnificent park and palace of the Bourbons, now freely open to the public, abundantly repay repeated visits. In fact, to attempt to see Versailles thoroughly in one visit is absurd. Neither pleasure nor benefit can be derived from sightseeing when the mind has become surfeited and the body wearied. At least one day should be devoted to the palace; a second to the park and its dependent villas,

—the Grand and Petit Trianons; and a third, after a little interval, to a review of the whole.

It has been calculated that if a tourist should give but five minutes to each apartment of this palace, it would take him three days, of five hours each (it is open only from eleven to four o'clock) to pass through the rooms; and that if he devoted but one minute to each work of art here, he would need seven days, of five hours each, to examine them. The entrance to the Palace of Versailles is worthy of its memories.

Passing two sentries at the gilded gate, one finds himself within a courtyard of immense proportions, well fitted for a grand display of military pageants and of royal retinues. Behind him is the town, before him an astonishing array of structures, united in a sort of crescent, the points of which advance to

EQUESTRIAN STATUE OF LOUIS XIV IN THE COURTYARD OF VERSAILLES.

meet him. Before these various buildings, which nevertheless form one vast edifice, are marble statues of illustrious Frenchmen; while in the centre of the area stands the grand equestrian figure of Louis Quatorze,—the royal founder of Versailles.

It is a mistake to inspect this palace with a crowd, or even with a companion who cares nothing for its history. While all the tourists who have been your fellow travelers in the hour's railway trip from Paris hurry across this courtyard, eager to see the sights and catch a return train, you will do well to pause and let these old walls tell you something of

their history.   Show them a little interest and sympathy, and
they will soon speak eloquently of their eventful past.   The
clock, for example, above the central balcony of this palace,
marked formerly, not the time of day, but the hour when the
last king of France had died; and after such an event, the
officer of the royal bedchamber appeared upon that balcony
and broke his
wand of office,
crying, "The
King is dead!"
Then, taking up
another wand,
he exclaimed:
"Long live the
King!"

MARIE ANTOINETTE.

Who can for-
get, too, that in
this courtyard
of Versailles oc-
curred, in Octo-
ber, 1789, one
of the earliest
and most signifi-
cant outbreaks
of the Revolu-
tion? Seating
ourselves upon
the balustrade in this historic area, we have but to turn our
heads to see the road on which the famished mob of men and
women made their way that day to this magnificent château
to demand bread of their King.   Some hours after they had
left Paris for this purpose, thousands of infuriated people had
assembled here, destitute alike of food and shelter.   The King
hastily convened a council, which held a session lasting far into

THE CHAPEL AT VERSAILLES.

the night, forgetting meantime, with characteristic imbecility, to fill the stomachs of the famished multitude. Bonfires were, therefore, lighted in this courtyard, at one of which a horse was partially roasted and devoured half-raw. It was three o'clock in the morning when the mob gained access to the palace. The young Queen, Marie Antoinette, worn out with terror and excitement, had just sunk into an uneasy sleep, when she was aroused by a dreadful clamor on the stair-

case, the discharge of guns, the clashing of swords, and the shouts of insurgents. Her faithful guards had only time, ere some of them were massacred, to cry to her: "Flee for your life!" She sprang from her bed, and rushed to the door leading to the King's apartments. To her dismay, she found it bolted on the other

MARIE ANTOINETTE'S BED.

side. With the energy of despair she knocked and called for help. Some moments passed, which seemed like hours, but finally she was admitted. Yet hardly was the door closed behind her when the mob with yells and imprecations, burst into the apartment she had left. Meantime the Queen, having gained the King's rooms, was secure from all imme-diate danger; for the royal troops had hastened to the rescue, and forced the assailants back into the courtyard. There all was uproar and excitement. The crowd was now enor-mously increased, and wild with hunger, cold, and sleeplessness

v. — 6

demanded, as with one voice, that the King should go back
with them to Paris.   With Louis in their midst, they thought

LAFAYETTE.

that their condition would be made
endurable.   The King, not daring
to resist, consented to return.   But
what of the Queen?   The multitude
distrusted her far more than they
did Louis.   A hundred miscreants
were at that moment thirsting for
her blood.   One man, however, had
the tact and energy to save her.   He
was the noble ally of America in our
own Revolution,—the bosom friend
of Washington,—the Marquis de Lafayette.   As General of
the National Guard, he now approached the Queen.

"Madame," he said; "his Majesty is going to Paris.
What will you do?"

"Go with the King," she instantly replied.

"Come, then, first with
me," said Lafayette, pointing to the window.

"What! to the balcony?"
she cried.

She had heard the threats
and curses of the mob, and
for a moment she recoiled;
but only for a moment.
Then the daughter of Maria
Theresa recovered herself.

"Well," she answered;
"even if it be to torture and
to death, I will go."   A mo-

THE DAUPHIN.

ment later, holding her little son and daughter by the hand,
she stepped out on the balcony.

Tranquil enough it now appears, but what a scene must all this have presented that October morning, a little more than a hundred years ago! As Marie Antoinette appeared here with her children, an involuntary murmur of admiration at her courage ran through the assembled multitude. Calmly she looked upon that sea of angry, agitated faces. It was the first time she had ever witnessed such a sight, but it was not to be the last. Pres-ently the cry arose: *"Pas d'enfants!"* [No children!] Ma-rie Antoinette therefore pushed them back and advanced alone to the balustrade. Folding her arms upon her breast, she stood there like a true daugh-ter of the Cæsars. Several guns

APARTMENT OF MARIE ANTOINETTE, VERSAILLES.

were pointed at her, but no shot was fired. Her hour had not yet come. At this moment Lafayette, then the idol of the nation, appeared beside her. He did not speak, for his voice could not have been heard. He did something better. He took the hand of Marie Antoinette and raised it reverently to his lips. The time was coming when an act like that would cost a man his head; but not yet. Lafayette, as it were, guar-anteed thus the good will of the Queen; and instantly the fickle multitude gave a tumultuous shout of *"Vive la Reine!"* For the time being Louis XVI and Marie Antoinette were saved.

These memories of the courtyard of Versailles are only typical of those which every part of this old palace brings before the thoughtful tourist. In fact, the entire building is now a national museum, designed to teach the history of France and to perpetuate its glories. King Louis Philippe deserves the everlasting gratitude of his countrymen for having thoroughly restored Versailles and given it to the

THE GALLERY OF BATTLES, VERSAILLES.

nation as a school of history. Its splendid rooms and corridors have thus not only been restored to their original beauty of decoration, but have been filled also with an immense number of paintings, statues, and historic mementos, illustrative of all the men and great events that have reflected honor on the name of France. Three million dollars is said to have been thus expended; and the result is without parallel in Europe. As a royal residence, Versailles was associated only with Louis XIV and his two successors, but

THE HALL OF THE TENNIS-COURT, VERSAILLES

as a national museum it illustrates the history of France from earliest times, and commemorates with painted canvas, sculptured marble, and enduring bronze all her great sovereigns, poets, warriors, and statesmen, from Charlemagne to Napoleon, from Rabelais to Voltaire, and from Catharine de' Medici to the Empress Eugénie.

Here one may see the famous tennis-court where, in 1789, the delegates of the people, excluded from the Representative Assembly, met, and took the following oath: " We solemnly swear never to separate, but to assemble wherever circumstances shall require, until the constitution of the kingdom is established on a solid basis."

THE OATH IN THE TENNIS-COURT.

This tennis-court of Versailles was, therefore, the cradle of French liberty. Yet within twenty-four hours these chosen representatives of twenty-five million people were driven from even this unsheltered place, the keeper of the court merely saying that the King's brother wished that day to use the tennis-ground for a game of ball! Does one ask why they did not force an entrance? Because the alleged excuse was only a pretense. Bayonets glittered all about the court and fifty thousand troops were close at hand.

Here, too, is the famous Hall of the Bull's Eye (so called from a large, oval window in the wall), which was the royal

THE GALLERY OF MIRRORS.

antechamber, where all who sought an audience with the King humbly awaited permission to approach him. Adjoining this also is the death - chamber of Louis XIV, into which, on the 1st of September, 1715, another King, who disregards rank and etiquette when he calls on his victim, made his way unannounced by lackey or by chamberlain, and claimed the "Grand Monarch" for his own. Here Louis' haughty face still greets us from the wall; and near it, with a silken covering embroidered by Madame de Maintenon, is the bed on which he breathed his last.

The most imposing hall in this old palace is its Gallery of Mirrors. It derives its name from the fact that one side of it, through its entire length of

HALL OF THE BULL'S EYE, VERSAILLES.

two hundred and forty feet, is lined with mirrors forty feet in
height and set in gilded frames.   Opposite to these are as
many lofty windows, commanding a fine view of the gardens
and fountains of Versailles.   What scenes of splendor and
renown would start forth from the walls if the grand mirrors
could give back the forms that have so often been reflected

NAPOLEON AT JENA, GALLERY OF BATTLES.

from their surfaces!   What would have been the feelings of
the former sovereigns of France — who never dreamed that
this imperial abode would shelter any dynasty but theirs —
could they have known that in this Gallery of Mirrors, during
the siege of Paris, the King of Prussia would be proclaimed
Emperor of united Germany; and that, as such, he would
receive here the homage of his subjects, the Crown Prince
being the first to bend the knee!

It is said that one travels seven miles in walking through the rooms and corridors of Versailles. The longest of its apartments is the Gallery of Battles. As one looks down its glittering perspective the effect is dazzling; for the floor, inlaid with variously colored woods, is beautifully polished; the roof is of glass, adorned with elaborate gilding; and the resplendent arches rest on marble columns, before which, on handsome pedestals, are busts of famous generals. But the

especial glory of this hall is its remarkable series of historical paintings—all of them admirable works of art—representing the victories of France, and, especially, the many battle-fields over which the genius of Napoleon has spread unfading glory. To the credit of the Germans be it said, that though Versailles was occupied many months by Prussian troops, these paintings, portraying as they do some terrible defeats inflicted on the Germans by Napoleon, were neither removed nor injured in

THE LAST DAYS OF NAPOLEON I.   *Vela.*

the least. Nay, more than this, these masterpieces of art were carefully covered and protected, and were found by the returning French as perfect as before.

Among the many objects in this national museum which suggest the past, none is more striking and impressive than Vela's admirable statue, entitled "The Last Days of Napoleon at St. Helena." This is indeed a masterpiece. It is not merely the dying Napoleon whom one here beholds. It is the exile, the dethroned Emperor, the heart broken captive, forgotten by those whom he had raised from the dust and

THE GALLERY OF BATTLES, VERSAILLES.

made illustrious, abandoned by his Austrian wife, deprived
of the means of communicating with his idolized child, and
stung by daily provocations from his English jailer.   Upon
his lap the outspread map of Europe lies beneath his
nerveless hand.   That hand once carved out empires there:
it is now powerless to trace his name.   To have been practically the sovereign of half of Europe; to have made and

THE PARK OF VERSAILLES.

unmade kings at will; to have outrivaled Cæsar in his victories; to have created an imperial dynasty, and then,—to lose
it all, yet linger on, chained like Prometheus to a barren rock,
his heart continually gnawed by the insatiable vulture of
regret: what tragedy has the world beheld to equal it?   Better
to fall, like the first Cæsar, beneath the daggers of conspirators, than to die by inches in captivity, as did the Cæsar of
the nineteenth century!

The immense park of Versailles, with its world-famous

THE FOUNTAINS AT VERSAILLES.

fountains and shaded avenues, groves, and lawns, peopled
with a multitude of statues, is still as beautiful naturally as
when its picturesque *allées* saw, like a company of actors on a
splendid stage, the brilliant court of Louis XIV; but even
more attractive (at least to the writer of these pages) is
that portion of it, known as Lit-
tle Trianon.   For, aside from the

LITTLE TRIANON.

beauty of rustic bridges, stately trees, and well-kept turf, the
grounds and buildings of Petit Trianon recall the joyous,
youthful life of Marie Antoinette.   This was her rural home,
whither she loved to retire when wearied of the tedious cere-
monials of the court.   In the neighboring palace of Versailles she was a Queen, weighed down with grave responsi-
bilities, and fettered by the numberless annoyances incident
to fashionable life.   But here she was a happy woman, wife,
and mother, discarding all formality, even to the extent of
ridiculing (unwisely as it proved) the rigid etiquette of old
French royalty.   Dressed in white muslin and wearing a
pretty straw hat trimmed with flowers, she strolled along
these shaded paths with careless grace, chased butterflies, fed
the chickens, fished in the tiny lake, or chatted with the
dairy-maids as freely as a peasant girl.   Upon these lawns
she introduced such games as " blind man's buff " and "fox
and geese," and joined in all their fun and frolic.   Private
theatricals were also very popular here, and the Queen took

IN " PETIT TRIANON."

part in them, assuming the character and costume of a shep-
herdess.

I do not know a pleasanter occupation on a summer afternoon than to come out from Paris and spend some hours at
Little Trianon, reading beneath the grand old trees, or wandering among the
modest buildings
once occupied by the
young Queen, her
husband, and their in-
timate friends. The
stone walls of these
pretty structures are
now covered with a
mantle of green ivy,
and moss has gath-
ered on the steps
once trodden by
those royal feet. It is
a fascinating though
melancholy task to

DISCARDING ALL FORMALITY.

search beneath these cold, deserted ashes for the few sparks
they possibly conceal. The rooms that echoed once so
frequently to joyous laughter are now empty and desolate,
abandoned to oblivion and silence. One cannot enter them.
The doors are locked. Peer through the windows, and from
the dark interior the reflection of your face will startle you,
as you think of other faces that these walls have seen,—faces
of brilliant men and lovely women, who nevertheless were
destined in a few short months to perish by the guillotine.
One of these buildings is the rustic mill where Louis XVI
assumed the rôle of miller, and shouldered heavy sacks of corn
while Marie Antoinette and her companions played the part
of peasants sitting on benches by their cottage doors.

Such freedom from restraint, however, was sharply criti-
cised by those who were not invited to participate in this
simple rural life.   Old courtiers expressed themselves as
amazed at such plebeian conduct, and the ceremonious dow-
agers of France were horrified at what they called the young
Queen's lack of propriety.   This feeling Marie Antoinette
recklessly resented, and even took the keenest pleasure in
shocking "Madame Etiquette," as she humorously styled the
first lady of her suite.   Thus, one day, in a donkey ride at
Trianon she had a fall.   Instead of rising, however, she
remained seated on the ground, and laughingly refused to
move until a lackey should bring Madame Etiquette, to tell
her the precise rule for a French Queen's getting up after a
tumble from a donkey.   This tendency of the young sovereign to ridicule her opponents led her imperial mother, Maria
Theresa, Empress
of Austria, to write
to her as follows:
"It reaches me
from every quarter
that you are not
particular to say
agreeable things
to people, but, on
the contrary, in-
dulge in ridicule.
This may do you
infinite harm.   By
amusing five or

THE HOME OF MARIE ANTOINETTE.

six young ladies or gentlemen, you may offend all others.
This is no slight fault in a princess, for it leads to imitation
on the part of her courtiers, and repels those who do not like
to have their feelings hurt.   If you are not careful, I foresee
great trouble for you.   I beg you, therefore, to take the

advice of a mother who knows the world, who idolizes her children, and whose only desire is to be of service to them." Admirable advice, indeed, but it was of little use. "*Si la jeunesse savait, si la vieillesse pouvait!*" [If youth only knew, if old age only could!] That is indeed a motto for all

THE DAIRY OF MARIE ANTOINETTE.

time. It is not strange that in return for some of Marie Antoinette's sharp pleasantries, sarcastic epigrams were made at her expense. One of these ran as follows:

> "Little Queen, you must not be
> So saucy with your twenty years;
> Else your subjects soon will see
> You led beyond the French frontiers."

At this time, also, Marie Antoinette was very fond of extravagant head-dresses. In one of these she had her portrait

painted, and sent it to her mother. But Maria Theresa
promptly returned it, with the words "I should have liked
exceedingly a portrait of the Queen of France; but since you
have made a mistake and sent   me that of
some *comédienne*, I return   it by
the first express."

Perhaps the most
interesting of the
buildings at Pe-
tit Trianon is
the little dairy
of Marie An-
toinette, where
cream was placed
in exquisite
porce-

THE MILL.

lain,
and milk
was skimmed
on marble ta-
bles by the fair
Queen and her
young friends,
many of whom
were soon to be be-
headed by the pop-
ulace. Innocent though
these pleasures were, they
did great harm to Marie

THE BOUDOIR AT TRIANON.

Antoinette; for there were many political intriguers at Versailles whose interest it was to injure her as much as possible, and her impatience of the restraints of royal etiquette

gave them an opportunity of doing so. Accordingly, each novel act of hers was called an innovation from Vienna, and she was nicknamed in reproach "The Austrian." Her enemies, too, watched eagerly for every indiscreet act and tried thereby to vilify her. The most outrageous calumnies were thus invented; and soon not merely France, but the whole of Europe was filled with stories of her improprieties. Maria Theresa was so disturbed by them that she privately sent a trustworthy friend to Paris to observe her daughter's conduct and report to her. But he presently wrote to her: "The young Queen is imprudent, that is all." Nevertheless, hundreds of songs were sung about her in the streets,

A CORNER OF THE CONCIERGERIE.

and so terrible were some of the stories circulated, and so readily were they believed, that Marie Antoinette became one of the most unhappy of women. There were times, doubtless, when she would gladly have exchanged the splendor of Versailles, and even the lovely groves of Trianon, for the lot of the humblest peasant in the furrowed field; for to be loved was to her the very breath of life—to be hated stabbed her to the heart. "One morning at Trianon," writes one of her biographers, "I entered the Queen's room and found her weeping bitterly. Some letters were lying near her, and her sobs were frequently interrupted with the words: 'Oh, how I wish that I were dead! Wretches! Monsters! What have I done to them? It would be better to kill me at once.'" It would have been better indeed; for these cruel calumnies were sharpening for Marie Antoinette the blade of the guillotine.

Seated among the trees of Little Trianon and looking on these empty and deserted buildings, one naturally thinks of that gloomy prison in the neighboring capital,—the Conciergerie. Within its walls there is one room which no one with a tender heart can look upon unmoved. It has been consecrated by great sorrow. When Marie Antoinette was imprisoned there, the Revolution had become a Reign of Terror. The power rested with the most abandoned. The King had already perished; and now the daughter of Maria Theresa was doomed. She was still a Queen, but they had driven her from her throne; a wife, but they had guillotined her husband; a mother, but they had robbed her of her children; a friend, but the gory head of her beloved companion, the Princesse de Lamballe, had been displayed beneath her window on a pike. Now she was only a poor woman, possessing nothing but her life. This also they resolved to have.

DANTON.

It was four o'clock in the morning when she arrived here from the Temple, where she had been long imprisoned. A tallow candle revealed a slimy floor, a filthy bed, a pine table, and a chair. The room itself measured only fifteen feet long and seven wide, yet part of this was reserved for a soldier who never left her, night or day. Her wardrobe now consisted of but two dresses, worn almost to rags; while her shoes and stockings were almost beyond the possibility of repair. Her hair was snow-white, though she was but thirty-seven. Such was the sequel to Versailles and Trianon!

It was a cold autumnal morning when Marie Antoinette was led from this prison to her execution. With her own hands she had cut off her hair. Then, with her arms secure-

MARIE ANTOINETTE IN THE CONCIERGERIE.

ly bound, she walked down through the prison with a guard of sol- diers. Outside the gateway was a hooting mob. Up the stone steps, however, the Queen ad- vanced as firm- ly as if she had been going to her throne. But alas! instead of a closed car- riage, as in the case of the King, only the open cart of the condemned awaited her. For a moment she recoiled from this unlooked-for degradation; but immediately recovering her composure, she took her seat in the cart.

It was in the Place de la Concorde, just in front of the entrance to the garden of the Tuileries, and with a view of the park and palace before her, that Marie Antoinette awaited death. She gazed in silence on these scenes of former hap- piness and grandeur, and a few tears rolled down her sunken cheeks. Then, turning toward the distant towers of the

MARIE ANTOINETTE GOING TO EXECUTION.

Temple, she murmured: "Farewell, my children; I go to rejoin your father." As she was led to the guillotine, she stepped, by accident, on the foot of the executioner. "Pray pardon me," she said, with as much courtesy as if she were at Versailles. A moment more, and the head of Marie Antoinette was held before the multitude. Upon the books of the parish of La Madeleine is this item of expense: "Coffin for Louis' widow, seven francs!"

Another interesting excursion to be made from Paris leads the tourist to the suburb of St. Denis. The principal object of attraction here is the old cathedral, which was for centuries a burial-

MARIE ANTOINETTE IN THE DEATH-CART.

place for the Kings of France. The place on which this building stands has been for sixteen hundred years a place of religious worship, a chapel having been erected here about the year 275, above the grave of St. Denis, the first bishop of Paris, who it is said suffered martyrdom on the Parisian hill of Montmartre, or the "Hill of Martyrs."

The present cathedral, though it has been frequently restored, is more than seven hundred years old, and would repay a visit, merely for its noble architecture and for its modern stained-glass windows, whose brilliant colors and noble figures suggest a high mass, visible, but inaudible.

No church in France had been so rich in relics and rare ornaments as this, and it contained the celebrated Oriflamme, or
consecrated banner of the kingdom. But that which gave
the church its greatest fame was its collection of royal tombs;

ST. DENIS.

for nearly all
the Kings of
France, togeth-
er with their
families, were
buried here up
to the time of
the Revolution.

In 1793, how-
ever, the Con-
vention decreed
that all these
sepulchres of
royalty should
be destroyed,
and on the
twelfth of October, in that year, the work of devastation
was begun. The populace, authorized by the decree of the
Convention, broke through the walls of the crypt, and dragging forth the bodies of the famous dead, some of which had
reposed there for a thousand years, threw them into a ditch
dug in the vicinity. A kind of madness seemed to have
seized upon the people who, drunk with the lust for blood
and pillage inspired by the massacres in Paris, hastened from
their capital to St. Denis. In their hatred of royalty and
their complete repudiation of the past, they did not seem to
realize that they were destroying proofs of their own national
history.

In their impatience to begin their evil deeds, they halted,
on their way to the cathedral, to desecrate twelve beautiful

wayside crosses, erected in the thirteenth century to commemorate the various places where the body of St. Louis
rested on its way from Paris to its royal tomb.

Pausing again at a smaller church, as if to prepare themselves for a greater act of sacrilege, they dragged from its
position over the high altar a famous wooden statue of the
Virgin, and, tying a rope around its neck, set it on fire and
watched it burn, dancing meantime around it and singing the
"Ça ira" and the "Carmagnole."

Finally, maddened with excitement, the crowd arrived
before the church of St. Denis, whose splendid bronze gates,
given to it by Charlemagne, were closed. Without a moment's hesitation, however, they attacked them with stones
and axes, and soon had broken to pieces one of the most
perfect relics of
early French art.
Then, rushing
within the sanc-
tuary, they at-
tacked the royal
tombs with the
same fury they
had shown in
tearing down the
gates of bronze.
They overthrew
the statues of
saints and Kings,
smashed the
stained - glass

ST. DENIS, INTERIOR.

windows, broke off the delicately sculptured ornaments of the
tombs, defiled the altars, and when they reached the coffins
themselves tore them open with a reckless vandalism tem-
pered only by curiosity and avarice. The skulls, bones, and

ashes of Kings, Queens, Princes, and Bishops, all of whom
had occupied prominent places in the history of France, were
tossed about and commented upon as vulgarly as if they had
been pebbles or potatoes. The head of Louis XII was kicked
about the pavement. One of the mob called the royal crypt
a "rat-hole," and the appellation was received with loud
applause. Amid the blows of axes could be heard the rib-

TOMBS OF LOUIS XII AND ANNE OF BRITTANY.

ald laughter of
those sacrileg-
ious vandals as
they pulled the
remains of a King
or Bishop from
his resting-place
and threw the
bones at each
other's heads.

However,
when they came
upon the coffin of
Henry IV, the
gallant Henry of
Navarre, even
these lawless ruf-

fians were somewhat impressed. He had been the most
popular of French Kings, and at first they were very careful
not to injure his body. It had been very skillfully embalmed
and wrapped in bands of linen, and when these were un-
rolled, to the surprise and almost terror of the spectators, the
corpse of the great King appeared almost as perfect as when
buried. The eyes were open, and the wounds made by the
knife of Ravaillac were distinctly visible. Presently, however, a reaction took place. Even this sovereign, who had
been the idol of the people, could not be then respected,

although sanctified by death, because *he had been a King!*
Accordingly one of the mob, placing himself in front of the
coffin, waved his red cap, and shouted to his fellows: "Come
patriots, be lively!   Let's get the old rascal out of the way,
and dig up the rest of the crowned brigands!"   These words
produced the desired effect, and the body of Henry IV was
immediately dragged from the church, thrown into the ditch,
and covered with lime.   Subsequently the body of Louis
XIV, the founder of Versailles, the "Grand Monarch" of
France, was also cast into the trench with the most revolting
disrespect.

By a curious coincidence, at the very hour when the
remains of Louis XV were flung head foremost into the ditch
at St. Denis, the mutilated body of Marie Antoinette was
thrown into a common grave in the cemetery of La Madeleine.

Much disappointment was experienced because so little
jewelry was found in these tombs, the exception being the
discovery of two vases of pure gold containing the hearts of a
son and a daughter-in-law of Louis XV.

When the coffin of Marshal Turenne was opened, his body
was discovered to be in a state of almost perfect preservation.
Hence, as it was about to be thrown into the pit with the
others, a representative of the medical faculty of France
stepped forward and demanded the corpse of the great soldier, that he might exhibit it in the Museum of Comparative
Anatomy as a "magnificent illustration of how a mummy
should be prepared."   The Marshal's body was, therefore,
handed over to this gentleman, who caused it to be trans-
ported to the Jardin des Plantes, where it remained for nine
years between the skeletons of a monkey and a camel!   This
scandal, in the course of time, being reported to Napoleon,
he ordered that the hero's body should be buried with military honors in the Invalides.

The horrible scenes of sacrilege at St. Denis lasted for

twelve days, and by that time the building was a ruin; the tombs were tenantless, the statues were mutilated, the splendid windows had been broken out, the high altar was desecrated, and as the roof had been stripped of its lead for

URN FOR THE HEART OF FRANCIS I.

bullets, the rain came freely through a hundred openings.

It was Napoleon I who ordered this grand edifice to be restored as nearly as possible to its former condition. Fortunately, a citizen named Alexandre Lenoir had obtained permission from the Government to gather together the fragments of the royal tombs and to exhibit them in a museum. Hence it was possible to restore quite a number of them. Napoleon III, in 1860, carried out still further the purpose of the great Emperor, and after the plans of Viollet-le-Duc completed the restoration of the building on a scale of great magnificence. Thus, each tomb has been either reconstructed or carefully restored, and placed in the position which it occupied before the Revolution. But, as it was impossible to distinguish and identify the ashes of the Kings, mixed as they were with the quicklime that consumed them, they were collected and buried *en masse* beneath the high altar, together with the supposed relics of Louis XVI and Marie Antoinette, conveyed here from the cemetery of La Madeleine.

If one could spend some hours quietly in this historic edifice, going from one tomb to another, and studying the different mausoleums with their elaborate canopies, reliefs, and statues, a visit to St. Denis would be of the greatest possible pleasure and advantage. Unfortunately, however, one is usually hurried through the building, with a crowd of tourists, by an attendant who rattles off in a perfunctory manner the names of the illustrious dead, the years of their reigns, and the names of the sculptors of their monuments. Yet even the most hasty visit here will leave upon the mind a deep impression, as one beholds these splendid monuments and statues, commemorating with pathetic irony those sovereigns of France, whose word decided once the fate of millions, yet whose remains were thrown into the ditch, and whose tombs are, therefore, little else than gorgeous cenotaphs.

As I emerged from this cathedral, and rode slowly back to the great capital, it seemed to me that I had never witnessed such a striking illustration of the vanity of human pride and power.

> "For those who husbanded the Golden grain
> And those who flung it to the winds like Rain,
> Alike to no such aureate Earth are turn'd
> As, buried once, Men want dug up again."

Twelve miles from Paris, in the little village of Rueil, is an estate of remarkable historical interest, which, nevertheless, is rarely visited by tourists. It is the ruined château of Malmaison, the home of Napoleon when First Consul, and the place where his divorced wife,

MALMAISON.

Josephine, breathed her last. On my first visit to Malmaison, the guardians of the estate were an old soldier of the empire and his white-haired wife, who seemed delighted that a stranger took sufficient interest in the château to come to it from Paris, and showed me through the edifice and its adjacent park with an eagerness and pride almost pathetic. The many recent memoirs of Napoleon I have brought this early home of his into more prominence; but until 1900 it

TREE AT MALMAISON PLANTED BY NAPOLEON AND JOSEPHINE.

was neglected.* Malmaison was never a palace; it was a simple country-house, whither the First Consul loved to retire in order to forget for a time the cares of State. Here he and Josephine received their friends in unaffected freedom, and frequently upon the spacious lawns, indulged in games like "blind man's buff," and "prisoner's base." The château itself has been allowed to fall into a state of great dilapidation. Its floors are disfigured, its walls defaced, and its ceilings broken. Yet the memory of Josephine still pervades the place, like the subtile perfume of which Moore so exquisitely sings:

> "You may break, you may shatter the vase if you will,
> But the scent of the roses will hang round it still."

One still beholds at Malmaison a tree planted by Napoleon and Josephine; and a long shaded avenue, called the

----

* In 1900, M. Osiris, of a prominent Jewish family of Paris, purchased the estate of Malmaison, and presented it to the State.

PONT DES ARTS AND THE INSTITUTE OF FRANCE.

"Promenade Solitaire," leads to a little summer-house where the First Consul planned many of the campaigns and dictated many of the decrees destined to change the face of Europe and the history of the world. I have never stayed any length of time in Paris without visiting Malmaison and strolling thoughtfully up and down this solitary path between old trees which formerly cast their shadows on the "Arbiter of Europe" as he walked back and forth in silent revery, or else conversed with the leading statesmen, soldiers, or scientists of France.

It was to Malmaison, where she had been so happy as the wife of the First Consul, that Josephine retired after the divorce. She

NAPOLEON'S STUDY AND PROMENADE SOLITAIRE.

came here, however, with the title of Empress, which she was permitted to retain, and an income of one hundred and twenty thousand dollars a year. For the Emperor insisted that she should maintain her former rank; and once, when he learned that she had been out driving without a uniformed escort, he reproved her. His courtiers also knew that one of the surest passports to his favor was a willingness to go to Malmaison and render homage to his wife, whom nothing but political motives had caused him to discard. Here, too, Josephine continued to receive from him affectionate letters and occasional visits, until disasters came upon him thick and fast. Their last interview took place in those cruel days in 1814, when France was invaded by Austrians, English, Prussians, Swedes, and Saxons. The military genius of the Emperor, though never seen to such advantage, could

JOSEPHINE.

do but little then to oppose the advancing flood. In ten days he had gained five victories over amazing odds, but overwhelming numbers made his struggles hopeless. In such a frame of mind, he came here for a hurried interview with his former wife. It was their last meeting. At its close the weary Emperor took her hand, and said: "Josephine, I have been as fortunate as any man ever was on this earth; but, in this hour, I have not in the whole wide world any one but you on whom I can rely."

Some months later, the duel between Napoleon and united Europe had ended, and the Emperor, after his first abdication, was a prisoner on the island of Elba. It was then that Josephine, astonished to learn that Marie Louise had not followed him into exile, wrote him from Malmaison that, if he desired it, she herself would go to him at once, since she was as thoroughly devoted to his interests as ever. Alas! a few weeks later she died here in the arms of her children Eugène and Hortense,—her last words being "The island of Elba—Napoleon." It is pathetic to remember that the last place visited by Napoleon before leaving Paris for St. Helena was Malmaison. It was after his defeat at Waterloo. His mighty empire was lost. His Austrian wife had abandoned him. His child was in the hands of his enemies. Even Josephine was dead. The world seemed crumbling beneath his feet. Speechless from grief, he walked about these grounds accompanied by Josephine's daughter, Hortense; but finally he requested her to leave him, and retired to the room

where Josephine had died, the year before, with his name on
her lips. He must have realized then that from the moment
he divorced Josephine his star had waned.

> "Ah, my poor Josephine! Alas! Alas!
> She gave her life a willing sacrifice;
> And I, with my own hands, tore out her heart
> And mine, and laid them bleeding on the shrine of France.
> But to what end? That the hell-hounds of Fate,
> . . . should lick the flames up
> From that altar's crest, to follow hot
> Upon my track forever after!"

In the village of Rueil, about a mile from Malmaison, is a
humble church in which reposes all that is mortal of the first
wife of Napoleon. One afternoon, as I approached it, its
bell was softly sending forth a call to prayer. I listened to
it with a mournful interest, remembering the words of Bour-
rienne, Napoleon's secretary, when he says: "The sound of a

bell produced an effect upon
Napoleon which I could
never explain. When we
were at Malmaison and were
walking in the road which
led to Rueil, how many
times has the sound of the
village church bell stopped
our most serious conversation! He would instantly
pause, that the noise of our
steps might not cause him
to lose a single one of those
distant tones which so delighted him."

TOMB OF JOSEPHINE, RUEIL.

Beside the altar of this church is the tomb of Josephine.
A graceful statue in spotless marble represents the Empress
kneeling in the attitude which she assumed, when waiting for

Napoleon to put the crown upon her head at the coronation ceremony in the cathedral of Notre Dame, so beautifully portrayed in David's famous painting.

It was on the 29th of May, the anniversary of her death, that I stood here, and saw fresh wreaths upon the railing of her tomb (among them, one sent by Eugénie from her place of exile), and on the pavement many lovely flowers, to which I added some that I had plucked at Malmaison.

Napoleon and Josephine,—how different are the sentiments which their memories inspire! Regarding one, the world's opinion is divided; for while by some Napoleon is adored, by others he is execrated. But there is little difference of opinion in regard to Josephine. The whole world gives to her its love and sympathy, and her noblest epitaph might be the words she spoke an hour before her death: "The first wife of Napoleon never caused a single tear to flow."

Whether an admirer of the great Emperor or not, every visitor to Paris goes to the tomb of Napoleon. It is one

of the most impressive monuments in the world. Above it is a stately dome whose richly gilded surface glitters in the sun at a height of more than three hundred feet. Within its shadow, on the other side, is the Hôtel des Invalides—a home where the veteran soldiers of France may end their days in peace. On crossing the threshold of this mausoleum,

THE CHAPEL OF THE INVALIDES.

the first impression of the place is awe-inspiring. It is a kind of temple, lined from floor to roof with spotless marble. Four marble piers uphold the mighty dome. Directly opposite the entrance rises a magnificent altar, which, with its lofty canopy,

is composed of variegated marble, bronze, and gold. The floor is of mosaic in elaborate designs. At the four corners of this grand enclosure are smaller marble-lined apartments, in two of which repose the brothers of the Emperor— Joseph and Jerome.

Midway between the entrance and the

THE DOME OF THE INVALIDES, COVERING NAPOLEON'S TOMB.

altar is a marble crypt, sixty-nine feet in diameter. Into its depths, from stained-glass windows in the roof, there falls a multitude of rainbow hues; and here, enveloped in an atmosphere of glory, stands the grand sarcophagus within which the great conqueror sleeps. The form that once shook Europe with its tread now lies here motionless. The brow upon which nations gazed to read their destiny is now untroubled by a frown. The eagle glance which once embraced the world is clouded by the film of death. The wildly-

ENTRANCE TO THE CRYPT.

beating heart is still at last. Not even the bugles of the recently victorious Prussians nor the thunders of their artillery could rouse him from his dreamless sleep.

Behind the altar, a curving flight of steps leads to the entrance of the crypt itself. It is a grandly impressive portal of black marble, with doors of massive bronze. Above these are inscribed in golden letters the pathetic words dictated by Napoleon at St. Helena: "I desire that my ashes may repose on the banks of the Seine, among the French people whom I have loved so well." On the right and left are the tombs of Duroc and Bertrand, two of Napoleon's dearest

THE ALTAR AND THE CRYPT.

A HALL IN THE GRAND TRIANON, VERSAILLES.

friends—one of
whom fell be-
side him on the
field of battle,
while the other
was among the
faithful few who
clung to the ex-
iled Emperor in
adversity, and
shared with him
his long captiv-
ity at St. Helena.
The sarcoph-
agus itself is of

THE RETURN OF NAPOLEON'S BODY FROM ST. HELENA.

red porphyry, twelve feet in length and six feet in breadth.
Beneath its dark green pedestal, the pavement of the crypt
is of marble mosaic in the form of a gigantic star, around

NAPOLEON'S TOMB.

which are in-
scribed names
which once elec-
trified the world
— Jena, Maren-
go, Austerlitz,
Rivoli, the Pyr-
amids, and many
more.

From certain
points of view
this grand sar-
cophagus seems
to be guarded
by the colossal
crucifix of gold,

which towers above it on the altar; but it is also guarded by its own inherent majesty. It is a significant fact, that, though Parisian vandals burned the Hôtel de Ville, set fire to the priceless Louvre, and made the Tuileries a heap of ruins, no ruthless hand applied the torch to this magnificent mauso-

leum of the Emperor, no lawless foot profaned the splendid circle of this solemn sepulchre.

Nothing is more impressive than the permanency of Napoleon's greatness. Year after year accusers rise, assail his memory, and pass away. But still the Vendôme Column towers above Paris, and still

THE EMPEROR'S TOMB.

its plates of bronze portray in beautiful relief his victories over united nations. His memory resembles a gigantic cliff emerging from the sea of time. The waves of calumny may break against it; the lightning's bolt of hatred may descend upon its brow; the cutting winds of sarcasm and malice may attack its surface; clouds of misunderstanding may conceal it; and even the disintegrating touch of Time may strive to mar its massiveness; but presently the waves are stilled, the tempest disappears, the mists all clear away, and lo! the cliff is there, serene and indestructible.

They err who deem adversity an injury to posthumous fame. The surest stepping-stone to immortality is martyrdom. When Cæsar fell beneath the daggers of conspirators, his spirit took its place among the stars. The exile of Napoleon was his apotheosis. The very remoteness of his prison-isle caused the minds of those who had for twenty years admired, loved, hated, feared, and fought the Emperor, to project upon the southern sky a figure of colossal size. Seen through the mists of years the harsher features of this figure became softened, his sufferings gave to it a halo, his brilliant genius gilded it with glory, and England furnished St. Helena for its pedestal.

LA BELLE FRANCE

THE PONT DU GARD.

La Belle FRANCE.

A LL European travelers go to Paris, yet few of them
know of France more than they see of it through a car
window, as they are whirled along the rails connecting the metropolis with Marseilles, Calais, or Geneva. In
France the splendor of the capital conceals the milder radiance of the country. Paris may be
compared, historically and polit-
ically, to a central sun, around which
all the other towns of France revolve
as satellites.

The capitals of Italy and Germany,
on the contrary, resemble constellations, whose luminaries
rival one another in respect to
brilliancy, while still maintain-
ing to each other the same rel-
ative position and importance.
The reason for this difference
is apparent. While France has
always been an undivided nation, with but one grand capital, both Italy and Germany

FRANCIS I.

have been till recently composed of numerous duchies, prin-
cipalities, and kingdoms, each having its own court, cathedrals, palaces, and art collections, besides the usual historical

prestige and architectural embellishment pertaining to an independent State. Thus, in Germany, Dresden, Berlin, Hanover, Munich, Stuttgart, and Weimar, and in Italy, Venice, Milan, Florence, Genoa, Pisa, Parma, Rome, and Naples were separate capitals for centuries, and as such, acquired an individuality in architecture, art, and history which makes a visit to them even now, when some of them have fallen into a

RURAL FRANCE.

subordinate rank, instructive and delightful. To neglect France, however, merely because her smaller cities cannot compare in interest with Paris, is a great mistake. Rouen, Bordeaux, Marseilles, Toulouse, Nîmes, Arles, and Avignon, all well repay a visit; her noble Pyrenees exhibit the most delightful mountain scenery in Europe, outside the region of the Alps; her Riviera has a charm in some respects unequaled in the world; and in the stately castles of her Kings and Emperors, all beautiful as works of art and eloquent of history, the thoughtful traveler will find a satisfaction and enjoyment hardly surpassed by anything that even Paris can afford.

An excursion in France that I never weary of making is that which takes one forty miles from Paris to the renowned Château of Fontainebleau. Among the various derivations of this castle's name, the most attractive is the one that finds

its origin in the words *Fontaine-belle-eau*, in consequence
of a limpid spring once highly prized by royal sportsmen.
At all events the name was sometimes used, for Henry IV
wrote to the charming Gabrielle d'Estrées a letter dated:
"From our lovely wilderness of *Fontaine-belle-eau*." The
history of France cannot be written without frequent mention
of this palace. Four of her Kings were born, and two have
died within its walls, and it has been a favorite abode of royalty for seven hundred years. Hence it may be compared to
a magnificently decorated volume of French history, each
page adorned with famous names, distinguished portraits,
regal coats of arms, and illustrations of the pageantry and
pleasure, luxury and intrigue, comedy and tragedy, insepar-
able from the records of a Court.

To one familiar with what has taken place here (and who
is not?), it is an impressive moment when he approaches the
château and steps within the area known as the Court of
Adieux. I felt, in doing so, that I was standing on a stage
from which the actors in a stirring drama had departed, leaving the curtain down, the lights extinguished, and the audience gone. The square lay sleeping in the sunshine of a
summer afternoon when I walked slowly for the first time
over the great blocks of stone that form its pavement, and
halted at the foot of the old "Horseshoe Staircase" leading

THE COURT OF ADIEUX, FONTAINEBLEAU.

to the entrance. I felt in no haste to mount the steps. In fact, I was not sure that the square itself was not enough to see and to reflect on in one day. It is true, these walls which have beheld so much of royal and imperial splendor are now silent, and these old steps so often trodden by the feet of men and women who can never be unknown to history are now abandoned to the tread of tourists; but must one for that reason pass them with a hasty glance nor pause to comprehend the story of their beauty and decay? The travelers who rush across the Court of Adieux and ascend these steps, eager to be the first admitted, in order to return that afternoon to Paris, do not appreciate Fontainebleau. But now and then a tourist comes to linger a few days at one of the hotels opposite the castle. He studies the historic palace leisurely and thoughtfully, as one sits down to contemplate a painting which others pass with but a hasty glance. He chooses for his visits to it hours before or after

HALL OF HENRY IV, FONTAINEBLEAU.

the arrival and departure of the crowd of sightseers from Paris. And in so doing he has his reward; for, as his imagination carries him back into the past, *he realizes history*. His former reading of French Courts and Kings seems based at last on facts whose import he had not before perceived. The sketches of historical characters which he had made in fancy and well-nigh forgotten, are suddenly reproduced by memory and placed here in appropriate frames; and he beholds again enacted in this court the scenes of former years, and hears its pavement echo to the tramp of horses' feet, to the gay music of the hunters' horns, or to the rumble of the royal carriages, as Francis I or Henry IV arrive here with a train of courtiers.

Among the many memories suggested by this courtyard, who can forget that of the 30th of March, 1814, when, at nine o'clock in the evening, a carriage drawn by four horses at full gallop entered its enclosure? Ten minutes before, a courier had preceded it, crying, as he alighted from his panting steed, "The Emperor! The Emperor!" While a

NAPOLEON AT FONTAINEBLEAU, 1814.

relay of fresh horses was being attached to the vehicle, Napoleon had time to inquire:

"Have you heard the sound of cannon during the day?"

"Yes, Sire."

"From which direction?"

"From that of Paris.'

"As I feared. When did it cease?"

"At five o'clock, Sire."

"To Paris!" cried the Emperor; and in an instant his carriage had resumed once more its impetuous course. An hour later he encountered an officer riding furiously toward Fontainebleau. He summoned him to halt, exchanged a few words with him, and then, in the same tone in which he had exclaimed "To Paris!" Napoleon cried to his postilions:

"Return to Fontainebleau." What he had learned was this:—Paris, at five o'clock that afternoon, had surrendered to the Allies.

Less than a month later, on the 20th of April, there was assembled in this square a body of men whose name had been for twenty years a synonym of courage and unparalleled devotion. It was the Old Guard of Napoleon, waiting to receive the farewell of their Emperor. These old companions of his many victories were still faithful to him. Unlike the marshals, courtiers, and innumerable beneficiaries of Napoleon, they had not received from him money, titles, and estates, which in the hour of his adversity they were afraid of losing. To these, his loyal grenadiers, whose tears fell silently upon their gray moustaches, he was their idol still, their "Little Corporal,"—the most successful soldier of the world. It was precisely one o'clock in the afternoon when the door at the head of the staircase was thrown open and there emerged upon the platform a solitary figure. It was he! The gray coat, the cocked hat, the classic silhouette of the Cæsars,—they knew them well, and were apparently never to see them more. Napoleon descended the steps, paused a moment, and then in a voice which revealed deep emotion, spoke these words: "Soldiers of my Old Guard, I bid you farewell. For twenty years I have always found you in the path of honor and glory. In these recent days, as in the time of our prosperity, you have not ceased to be models of courage and fidelity. With such

THE LAST REVIEW.

men as you our cause was not lost; but the war would have been interminable. It would have become civil war, and by it France would have been rendered even more unhappy. I have, therefore, sacrificed all our personal interests to those of our country. I must now depart; but do you, my friends, continue to serve France. Do not pity my fate. If I have consented to live on, it is to contribute still further to your glory. I wish to record the great deeds we have achieved together. Adieu, my children. I wish that I could press you all to my heart; but let me at least once more embrace your standard."
Here his voice faltered, and the flag which he held to his face concealed

THE TABLE ON WHICH THE ABDICATION WAS SIGNED.

his tears. At length his tones were heard again. "Farewell once more, my old companions," he exclaimed; then, embracing the eagle which surmounted the standard, he added: "May this last kiss penetrate your hearts." A moment later, amid the sobs of his veterans, Napoleon stepped into the carriage which awaited him and was driven away to live in exile on the island of Elba.

Who does not recollect the admirable painting of this scene by Horace Vernet, which now adorns the gallery of Versailles?

This courtyard is not the only portion of the palace associated with Napoleon. In one room, called the Cabinet de l'Abdication, still stands a round mahogany table on which, upon a sheet of paper that has since mysteriously disappeared Napoleon traced these words:

"The Allied Powers having proclaimed that the Emperor was the sole obstacle to the reëstablishment of peace in Europe, the Emperor, faithful to his oath, declares that he  renounces for himself and children the thrones of France and Italy, and that there is no sacrifice, even that of his life, that he is not ready to make for the interests of France." After the restoration, the Bourbons caused a copper plate to be at-

NAPOLEON'S BED, FONTAINEBLEAU.

tached to the lower side of this table, bearing the ridiculous inscription: "On the 5th of April, 1814, Napoleon Buonaparte signed his abdication upon this table in the King's study."

Another apartment closely connected with these scenes is the bedroom of Napoleon. It was here that the defeated monarch passed the awful hours previous to his abdication. For notwithstanding his tremendous efforts in the duel between France and allied Europe which ensued after the Russian campaign, the odds against him had been overwhelming. It is true, in the last months of the unequal

struggle, wherever he had been there had been victory, but
on the other hand, wherever he was not there was defeat.
Napoleon felt his empire slipping from his grasp. To crown
all, the Allies had declared they would not treat with him on
any terms save abdication. Put to that test, his marshals,
ministers, and courtiers, who feared to lose the titles, riches,
and estates which he had given them, left him as rats desert
a sinking ship. After being in the ascendant for nearly
twenty years, Napoleon's star seemed sinking here into an
ocean of ingratitude and treachery. Under these circumstances one can not wonder that the horror of his situation
drove him to despair. Pierced to the heart by the desertion
of men who owed to him everything they had and were, and
should have formed a rampart round him with their bodies,
Napoleon here attempted suicide. During the night of the
12th of April, the few remaining attendants of the palace
were aroused by cries and exclamations. They hastened to
the bedroom of the Emperor, but were refused admittance.
Only General Bertrand, Caulaincourt, the Duke of Bassano,
and the Emperor's physician Ivan were closeted with Napoleon. Suddenly the door opened, and Ivan, deathly pale,
rushed down the staircase to the courtyard, mounted a horse
and disappeared in the darkness like a madman. This was
because Napoleon, writhing in pain upon the bed we may still
see at Fontainebleau, had said to him: "Ivan, the poison
you gave me has produced no effect." In fact, during the
retreat from Moscow, Napoleon had ordered his physician to
prepare for him a poison, to prevent his falling alive into the
hands of the Cossacks. This the disheartened Emperor, dis-
gusted with ingratitude and treachery, took on that eventful
night at Fontainebleau, but it had so far lost its strength,
that it was powerless to destroy life.

Turning to the faithful friends who hastened to his bed-
side, Bonaparte murmured sadly: "Alas! everything betrays

me now, even poison." It was true. Death shunned him
here, as it had done upon the battle-field. Sad as his situation then appeared, it was nevertheless well that he could not
foresee the future; for in Napoleon's book of destiny two

NAPOLEON'S THRONE AT FONTAINEBLEAU.

pages still remained unturned. On one of them was inscribed
Waterloo and on the other St. Helena.

It was at Fontainebleau that Napoleon for the first time
spoke to Josephine of the necessity of a divorce. Standing in
the dining-room, one thinks of that ill-fated day, precursor
of so much misfortune. It was the 30th of November, 1809.
Napoleon and Josephine dined here alone and in almost

NAPOLEON AND JOSEPHINE IN THE SILK MANUFACTORY AT LYONS.

unbroken silence. In his memoirs, Constant testifies that they ate nothing, and that the only sounds heard during the repast were those of the dishes, brought and removed, and the tinkling of the Emperor's knife which he mechanically struck against his glass. At the conclusion of this mournful ceremony they entered the adjoining salon and were alone. After some minutes shrieks were heard. Constant was called.

The Empress was on the floor, weeping and exclaiming hysterically, " No, you will not do it! You do not want to kill me!"

When she had been carried to her bedchamber by her husband and an attendant, the Emperor rang for her servants,

BEDROOM OF THE EMPRESS JOSEPHINE, FONTAINEBLEAU.

and, on their arrival, retired in the deepest mental distress. Moreover, during the sleepless night that followed, he rose repeatedly to inquire after his wife's health, and his valet declares that he never saw him in such affliction. It is this suffering on the part of both that makes the separation of Napoleon and Josephine peculiarly pathetic. Despite some serious faults, Josephine was the only woman whom Napoleon ever really loved. It is a proof of his natural tenderness of heart that, steadily resisting the arguments and appeals of his own family, as well as those of the leading statesmen of France, he refused for years to entertain the thought of separation from his wife. Renouncing the natural longing of a father's heart for a son to follow him in a career of glory, he chose at first his brother's child to be his political heir, and only on the death of that little prince did he allow the subject of divorce to be reopened. For the question who should govern the colossal empire after his death was of such paramount importance that it could not be ignored. To secure an heir, and thereby found a permanent dynasty, and by marrying into one of the royal families to put an end to the continual coalitions against him, or to secure at least one ally, these, and not a lack of affection, formed the true

THE COUNCIL HALL, FONTAINEBLEAU.

reason for Napoleon's conduct. And when at last Josephine acknowledged and accepted the necessity of the sacrifice required, Napoleon's treatment of her, not only in generosity, but in delicate and reiterated proofs of continued friendship, is unsurpassed in either public or private history

Not far from the apartments of Napoleon one enters the elaborately decorated rooms occupied by Pope Pius VII on the two occasions when he visited Fontainebleau,—the first time as the Emperor's guest, the second as his prisoner. The Pope owed much to Bonaparte for having restored religion to the French nation. The Revolution had demoralized France. For years she had neither had a Sabbath nor recognized a God. Her churches had been closed and desecrated, and hundreds of priests were languishing in prisons. "No nation can exist without religion," said Napoleon; and straightway caused religious worship to be reëstablished throughout France. Opening the dungeon doors he also gave the imprisoned

priests their liberty, and bade them go to work again, reclaiming men from sin. In this, however, there was no intolerance, for he proclaimed that not an individual in France, whether Protestant,

ROOMS OF PIUS VII AT FONTAINEBLEAU.

Catholic, or Jew, should be molested on account of his religion. Still, notwithstanding these beneficent decrees of the First Consul, it was a wonderful act of condescension on the part of a Pope, for the first time in the history of Christendom, to leave the Vatican and travel hundreds of miles into a foreign land to crown Napoleon Emperor of France. Nevertheless,

the first visit of Pius VII, made for this purpose, was emi-
nently satisfactory, and on his return from Fontainebleau to
Rome he said: "I went to seek religion and I found it. I
traversed France through a kneeling people."

But, nine years later, when Napoleon, thus consecrated by
the Pope, had become practically sovereign of Europe, Pius
VII, having refused to give up to him the temporal power of
the Papal States, was by his orders brought from Rome to

HALL OF FRANCIS I, FONTAINEBLEAU.

Fontainebleau, a
captive. This time,
within these rooms,
furnished with so
much elegance, the
Pontiff lived like
an ascetic, spending
his days in fasting
and prayer. One
thinks here of the
stormy interviews
which must have
taken place be-
tween the all-pow-
erful Emperor and

his prisoner, for during many months the Holy Father would
not yield either to the threats or entreaties of Napoleon.
Finally, however, on the 19th of January, 1813, after a scene
in this apartment, the details of which still remain a mystery,
Pius VII consented to renounce his temporal sovereignty.
Some have declared that Bonaparte on this occasion became
so excited that he used personal violence towards the vener-
able Pontiff; but this, besides being extremely improbable,
was emphatically denied by the Pope himself.

There is a melancholy pleasure in strolling through
apartments that are haunted by such memories as these.

One after another, we enter and study them as separate chap
ters of French history.   A name recalled here almost as frequently as Napoleon's is that of Francis I, the pleasure-loving friend of artists, who called from Italy to Fontainebleau,
to aid in its embellishment, Leonardo da Vinci, Benvenuto
Cellini, Andrea del Sarto, Primaticcio, and Rosso.   Unfortunately Fontainebleau's souvenirs of the illustrious painter of
the Last Supper are few in number; for when Leonardo came
to the French Court he was sixty-three years old and in
feeble health, and consequently unable to contribute much
to art in the four years of life remaining to him.   The story
that he died in the arms of Francis is probably a myth, the
evidence being almost certain that the King was in another part
of France when Leonardo's death occurred; but that Francis I
always treated him with the greatest honor, and evinced sin-
cere grief on hearing of his death, there is no doubt.   In fact,
all the great geniuses of Italy whom Francis summoned here
were treated like princes; and sumptuous apartments, numerous servants, horses, hounds,—in short, the best the Court
afforded in the way of pleasure and of luxury,—were placed
at their disposal.   To Cellini Francis is said to have
exclaimed: "My friend, which is happier, the King who finds
an artist like yourself, or the artist who meets a King like
Francis I?"

In walking through these brilliant halls of Fontainebleau
we recollect the account of a visit paid here to the French
King, in 1539, by the redoubtable Charles V of Spain, who
wished to pass thus to the Netherlands through the kingdom
of his rival.

"If Charles dares to traverse France," said the King's
jester, "I will give him my fool's cap."

"But what if I allow him to do so?" asked the King.

"Then," replied the fool, "I will take back my cap and
make a present of it to you."

v. — 10

Francis I laughed, but Charles V came, was entertained extravagantly, and departed in safety.

Not without risk, however. For it is said that when Charles V first entered Fontainebleau, and was received by the French King, the beautiful Duchess of Étampes whispered to Francis, on whose arm she was leaning:

"Do not let him escape you."

"My brother," said Francis, a moment later, as he presented the duchess to his royal guest, "this fair lady has just advised me to keep you here a prisoner till you shall have destroyed the treaty of Madrid."

"If the advice is good," replied Charles V, "you should follow it;" and he proceeded to converse with his host as unconcernedly as if the latter had spoken merely in jest.

THE BALL-ROOM, FONTAINEBLEAU.

But two hours later, as they were about to seat themselves at table, and as the Duchess of Étampes presented to Charles V a gold basin containing water, the Spanish sovereign, as he dipped his hands in the liquid, dropped in the basin a diamond ring of great value. The duchess called his attention to it, but Charles V remarked smilingly: "The ring evidently wishes to change owners, and at present it is in too beautiful a hand for me to reclaim it." From that moment,

it is said, the duchess changed her policy, and far from urging
the King to treat the royal traveler treacherously, it was she,
who five years later, betrayed to Charles V the plans of Francis I, in the war then being waged between them.

In the long
library at Fon-
tainebleau,
called the Gal-
lery of Diana,
the traveler sees
a blood-stained
coat of mail
which, though
it turned at
first the sword-
thrusts of assas-
sins, could not
protect its wear-
er's life. The
sight of it recalls

THE LIBRARY, FONTAINEBLEAU.

an atrocious act of cruelty committed here by a woman.

On the 10th of November, 1657, Christina, ex-Queen of
Sweden, who was then residing at Fontainebleau, as a guest
of Louis XIV, having become convinced of the treason and
unfaithfulness of her favorite, the Marquis de Monaldeschi,
caused him to be murdered in the Galerie des Cerfs, an apartment just beneath the library. Her wretched victim flung
himself on his knees at her feet and implored her pardon, but
she was inexorable.

> "Heaven has no rage like love to hatred turned,
> Nor hell a fury like a woman scorned."

In a firm voice she remarked to the priest whom she had
summoned to absolve him, "My father, I now retire, leaving
this man to you. Prepare him for death and take care of his

soul." The priest himself then intervened with tears and sobs, but the woman was as unyielding and pitiless as stone. Half an hour later, the three swordsmen who had been ordered by Christina to despatch the prisoner announced to her that the deed was done. Louis XIV, then at Versailles, merely expressed displeasure at this murder, committed thus auda-

ALONG THE LOIRE.

ciously in one of his palaces, but Christina continued to remain here for nearly two years.

Midway between Paris and the Pyrenees there is a charming section of La Belle France, dotted with fertile vineyards, peaceful streams, picturesque castles, and historic towns, and known as La Touraine. Across this, like a silver girdle, stretches the river Loire, flowing along as peacefully as if its waves had not run red with blood and its broad valley had not often been the scenes of intrigues, wars, and massacres.

It is a singular river, apparently as capricious as some stately beauty of the old Court days, —now gathering up the blue folds of its current till the glistening pebbles are scarce visible, then dropping them again and sweeping on in slow, majestic curves, displaying proudly its long silvery train. In close proximity to this are several famous cas-

STATUE OF LOUIS XII, CHÂTEAU OF BLOIS.

tles which sovereigns of France have made their favorite abodes. The first of these which I beheld, one summer on my way to Spain, was the Château of Blois. The entrance is a sculptured portal, the sight of which seemed to transport me at once into the heart of the Middle Ages, for, with its elaborately carved columns, ornaments, and arches, it stood before me like some rare mediæval volume, with covers of the richest carving, and pages glowing with illuminated parchment and

A CORRIDOR AT FONTAINEBLEAU.

quaintly devised capitals. This castle has, in fact, been for centuries the residence of Kings and Princes, and the scene of many memorable events. Here was born Louis XII, whose equestrian statue crowns the doorway; hither was sent, as Florentine ambassador, the cunning statesman and unprincipled diplomatist, Machiavelli; here also Catharine de' Medici plotted deeds of blood; and to this Château of Blois, in 1814,

A PART OF THE STAIRCASE AT BLOIS.

came, in their flight from Paris, Marie Louise and the little King of Rome, when the allied armies of Europe were closing fast upon the capital, and Napoleon's mighty power was drawing near its end. Still other memories crowd upon the thoughtful tourist, who makes his way beneath this gate and enters the famous Court of Honor; for here his gaze immediately rests with admiration upon the principal architectural glory of the place,—the beautiful staircase of Francis I. This exquisite structure rises to the height of four stories, and is composed of stone so wonderfully carved and ornamented, that one might almost fancy that the docile mass had shaped itself, like sculptor's clay, beneath the fingers of the architect, obeying every caprice of his imagination. Or one might fancy it a fountain suddenly petrified and standing just as it was stopped in its joyous progress from the pavement.

Beautiful as it is, how-
ever, there is a deeper
pleasure here than that
which appeals merely
to the eye; for, let but
our imaginations carry
us back into the past,
and immediately the
scenes of by-gone days
start forth in vivid col-
ors from these old walls,
and we can almost hear
this staircase once more
echo to the tread of
mailed knights, the

THE STAIRCASE AT BLOIS.

music of sweet-voiced minstrels, and the laughter of lovely
women, like Diana of Poitiers, who once looked forth from
these same windows, whose jeweled fingers rested on these
very balustrades, and whose distinguished beauty gave to this
famous court a greater charm. So realistic also is the power

THE WARNING.

of genius, that we recall Dumas' " Three Guardsmen " here,
and, in imagination see those dashing musketeers drinking
and fencing in this castle, as the great novelist has described
them; for they seem like historical characters.   In lingering
on these steps, however, and tracing the dramatic chronicles
of France indelibly inscribed upon the walls, we sometimes
shudder, as we read the record.   Thus, in a room whose

THE MURDER OF THE DUKE OF GUISE.

windows open on this court, on the third night before Christ-
mas in the year 1588, the cowardly king Henry III sat plot-
ting the death of his enemy, the Duke of Guise, whom he had
ordered to appear before him at six o'clock the next morning.
The duke was not without repeated warnings of his danger.
At supper, on the previous evening, he had found in his nap-
kin a note with the mysterious words: "*Be on your guard!
A plot is formed against you!*"   But he threw it contemptu-
ously beneath the table, muttering, "They would not dare!"
The following morning, also, as the duke passed through

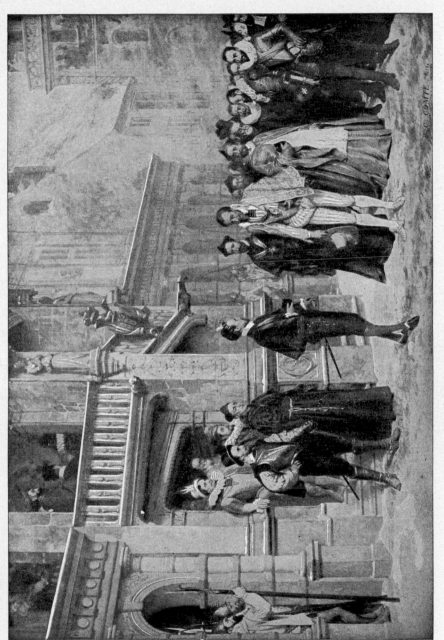

THE MEETING OF THE KING AND THE DUKE OF GUISE AT BLOIS

this court in the gray light of that December dawn, a woman's form appeared in a half-opened doorway, a white hand beckoned to him appealingly, and a voice, whose accents thrilled him, whispered from lips, trembling and white with fear: "Escape or thou art lost!" His only answer was a smile and a caressing gesture of assurance; then he passed proudly on into the Salle des Gardes.

It was a frosty morning, and a fire was blazing on the hearth. Complaining of the cold, the Duke of Guise leaned against the chimney-piece, and warmed his hands. Meanwhile in an adjoining room the King was putting daggers into the hands of forty-five assassins and ordering them to do his evil will. Presently a messenger summoned the duke to the royal presence. Guise rose, bowed to the company with his accustomed grace, and passed into the antechamber of the King.

DUKE OF GUISE.

Hardly had the door closed behind him, when his murderers fell upon him from behind the tapestry. He had just time to cry: "*À moi, mes amis!*"—but it was too late for friends to come to him. The door was locked; the murderers had him to themselves. He fought with his usual desperate courage, but he was only one against forty-five, and soon fell pierced with a hundred wounds. During the progress of this murder prayers were being offered up for its success in the adjoining chapel, and two hours later, the King, emerging from his apartment, looked on the prostrate body of his enemy, and spurning it with his foot remarked with cruel composure: "I did not think he was so tall." On the

CASTLE OF CHINON.

following day, the brother of the murdered man was likewise slain here by assassins; the two bodies being subsequently burned, and their ashes scattered on the surface of the Loire, lest any of their party should preserve them as a relic.

Yet speedy retribution followed these atrocious deeds. Only twelve days after these assassinations, the King's mother, Catharine de' Medici, the instigator of the crime, died beneath this roof in the ravings of delirium; and before eight months had passed, the weak and cruel sovereign himself perished at the hand of an assassin.

Making Blois our headquarters for a little excursion through Touraine, we found within easy distance of each other, several other castles of French royalty scarcely less interesting historically, and even more imposing architecturally, than the château which saw the murder of the Guises. Amboise, where rest the remains of Leonardo da Vinci, and which received fair Mary Stuart as the youthful bride of Francis II; Chinon, associated with the early scenes in the career of Joan of Arc, as she rode out across its drawbridge, clad in full armor, with her enthusiastic followers behind her, to conquer England's hitherto victorious army; Plessis, the haunt of the cowardly tyrant, Louis XI, so well described by Scott in Quentin Durward; Fontevrault, where Richard the Lionhearted breathed his last; Chenonceaux, the charming residence of Diana of Poitiers; Azay-le-Rideau, one of the most elegant specimens of sixteenth-century architecture in France; and Chambord with its marvelous exterior,— all these possess for the thoughtful tourist a fascination which harmonizes well with that charming country, where, Balzac declared, "In spring love flies at large beneath the open sky," and "In autumn the air is full of memories of those who are no more."

Time fails us to examine all these sculptured monuments of old French history, but two of them at least cannot be passed with a mere mention of their names. One of these,— the Castle of Chambord—is so near Blois that we drove to it easily in two hours, crossing

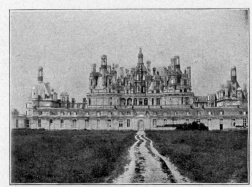

CASTLE OF CHAMBORD.

the Loire by a handsome bridge of stone, and winding thence for twelve miles through innumerable vineyards. The château itself, which might be called the Versailles of Touraine, is one of the most extraordinary edifices I have ever seen.

Our way to it led through a now deserted, melancholy park, twenty-one miles in circuit. Suddenly, at the end of a long avenue, we saw a vast bewildering conglomeration of huge round towers, turrets, spires, chimneys, gables, pinnacles, and gargoyles, rising like some great architectural flower, surmounted by one central tower, like the stamen of a lily, which itself terminates in a fleur-de-lis in stone six feet in height. In looking at its vast proportions and fantastic architecture, I comprehended why, in the period of its glory, it was compared to a palace of the Arabian Nights, springing from the earth at the stroke of some enchanter's wand. Chambord was built by the extravagantly capricious monarch, Francis I, who laid its foundation-stone in 1526, and employed eighteen hundred men for twelve years working continually in its construction, yet at his death was obliged to hand it over to his successor still unfinished. There are within this castle no less than thirteen spacious staircases of stone, to say nothing of small and secret ones, besides four hundred and forty rooms and several halls of state, one of which was, in the reign of Louis XIV, transformed into a theatre, where was performed for the first time Molière's "Bourgeois Gentilhomme," the author himself appearing on the stage. Here also is a famous double staircase, one series of steps being so arranged inside of the other that different parties can

A FIREPLACE AT CHAMBORD.

ascend it or descend it at the same time, without meeting, and almost without seeing each other.   This castle in its present loveliness seems as much of an anachronism as was the white flag of the Bourbons which the Count de Chambord (then the owner of the estate) wished to restore to France in 1871, in place of the tricolor, glorious standard of the Revolution and the Empire. So useless now are its elaborately decorated but tenantless apartments that there appears to be no reason for its further preservation.   Unlike the palace of Versailles, which has been made a national museum, Chambord seems only to recall by contrast the brilliant days when it was the magnificent abode of Francis I, who said of it: "A Court without women is like a year without springtime, or a springtime without flowers."   Yet it was on a window of this castle that Francis is said to have cut with a diamond his well-known lines on the fickleness of women:

CASTLE OF CHAMBORD.

> "Souvent femme varie,
> Fol qui s'y fie." *

Another castle of Touraine that well repays a visit is Chenonceaux.   The lovely site of this château, beside the river Cher, seems to have been appreciated and enjoyed ever

---

* Another version reads:
> "Toute femme varie,
> Mal habil qui s'y fie."

since the days of the Romans, but the edifice itself dates from
the early part of the sixteenth century, about the time when

CHENONCEAUX AND THE RIVER CHER.

Chambord and
a part of Fon-
tainebleau were
built. King
Henry II, son
of Francis I,
gave this estate
to his beauti-
ful favorite, Di-
ana of Poitiers,
whose name is more closely associated with it than that of
any other woman who has been its chatelaine. Her beauty,
like that of this château, seems to have triumphed over time,
for Brantôme, who saw her in her old age, declared that she
was then "as lovely, fresh and amiable as at the age of
thirty." Fair Mary Queen of Scots has also left at Chenonceaux some mementos of her youth and beauty, when she

resided here as
the bride of
her first hus-
band Francis
II. How little
could she dream
of the tragedy
the future held
in store for her,
as she looked
down upon this
peaceful river

CASTLE OF CHENONCEAUX.

gliding beneath the castle walls! As little as the stream itself
recks of the fearful storms that sweep the ocean whither it is
inevitably moving on.

Other châteaux of France have more historical associations than fair Chenonceaux, but few possess more beauty or are more eloquent of sentiment. For this, like Petit Trianon, was built for love; and wine, women, and song were the chief affairs of the life that slipped away here, swiftly and smoothly, like the river Cher. The interior of Chenonceaux is well preserved and has been carefully restored. It is especially fortunate in having escaped the devastation of the Revolution, and it still retains much of its ancient furniture, cabinets, china, glass, and tapestry. Among the relics of its former splendor is the mirror

A FIREPLACE AT CHENONCEAUX.

which once reflected the lovely features of Mary Queen of Scots.   It is interesting, too, to remember here that Chenonceaux, in the latter part of the eighteenth century, became a rendezvous for the distinguished literary men of France, invited hither by the owner of the castle at that time, the witty and attractive Madame Dupin. Among them, Voltaire, Rousseau, Buffon, and Diderot were her frequent visitors.

It would be a mistake, in studying the history of France to ignore the influence which women have exerted there. In explanation of how many political events might be uttered the words: *Cherchez la femme!* Whether as native favorites or imported Queens, women have often governed France as really, if not as openly, as the reigning monarch. Even without going back to the Middle Ages, we find in the sixteenth century the Duchesse d'Étampes, Diana of Poitiers, and Catharine de' Medici; in the

THE DONJON OF CHENONCEAUX.

seventeenth, Marie de' Medici, Madame de Montespan, and Madame de Maintenon; in the eighteenth, Madame de Pompadour, Madame du Barry, and Marie Antoinette; and in our time the influence of the Empress Eugénie on the reign of Napoleon III is incontestable. The French *salon* has always been a great political power in France; for as Napoleon dreaded the coterie of gossip and conspiracy patronized by

CHÂTEAU OF AZAY-LE-RIDEAU.

TOMB OF RICHELIEU, PARIS

Madame de Staël, so Richelieu was wont to say that the *petit salon* of Mademoiselle de Lafayette often caused him more anxiety than all the rest of Europe.

The castles of Touraine which still exist are few in number, compared with all the beautiful châteaux that once adorned this valley, for many such abodes of the no-

OLD FRENCH HOUSES.

bility were either destroyed or abandoned when Richelieu had concentrated the national power in the hands of royalty, and had compelled the feudal lords of France to yield unquestioning obedience to the King. Still, though the time had come for them to disappear, those castles had performed

THE RIVER GARONNE AT BORDEAUX.

a useful part in the process of national growth and civilization.

The mediæval fortresses of Europe should not be looked upon as merely the luxurious abodes of kings and nobles. They were the necessary outgrowth of that time. Foreign invasions and civil and religious wars made castles a necessity. Defenseless people were only too thankful then to rally around any powerful chief who built a stronghold and offered them protection. The owners of these castles were, therefore, almost independent sovereigns in their localities, and this gave rise to feudalism, which gradually yielded to the central royal power, as France became a homogeneous nation.

Leaving Touraine, with its old castles and historic memories, we halted next in our southward journey toward the Pyrenees, at Bordeaux. *Bord-d'eaux*, if not the accepted derivation of its name, would still be a very appropriate title for this city, lying on the border of the Garonne river, which, as it sweeps around

THE GRAND OPERA HOUSE, BORDEAUX.

the town in a majestic curve three miles in length, has a breadth of two thousand feet. Few cities in the world have such a water-front and such substantial quays as Bordeaux can display, and one can well believe its commerce fully justifies all that has been expended here in its embankments and magnificent bridge,— the handsomest in France. Bordeaux is, of course, preëminently the city of Bacchus, and on the altar of that deity are poured libations of those products of French vineyards which come to us across the ocean under such

BORDEAUX.

well - known labels as Château Margaux, Château Lafitte, Château Latour, Pontet Canet, St. Julien, and Médoc. The latter name, indeed, is given primarily to a long strip of grape - produc-cing land extending northward from Bordeaux between the ocean and the river, and this, in autumn, is loaded with innumerable clusters of the delicious fruit that is to send its flavor through the world.

> "Why, be this Juice the growth of God, who dare
> Blaspheme the twisted tendril as a Snare?
> A Blessing, we should use it, should we not?
> And if a Curse, why, then, Who set it there?"

The soil of Médoc is a light gravel which seems peculiarly adapted to the vine, because it retains the sun's heat about its roots for a long time after sunset. Bordeaux is not a city where the passing tourist will care to linger, but its hotels are comfortable, the view of its noble river, crowded with shipping, is exceedingly picturesque, and its Grand Opera House is one of the most imposing structures of the kind in Europe.

The form of the western coasts of France and Spain resembles that of a gigantic chair, and almost exactly at the point of union of its seat and back is situated Biarritz, fronting upon the Bay of Biscay.

"The winds are rude in Biscay's sleepless bay,"

says Byron, and in truth the roughness of that body of water has become proverbial. The ceaseless swell of the Atlantic pours into this peculiar area, formed by the huge projections of two countries, an uninterrupted series of enormous waves, which in recoiling from the sharp, rectangular coast lines are of necessity thrown into great confusion. Such billows have, in the course of ages, ravaged and honeycombed the opposing cliffs, beating them down and cutting them away from the mainland, so that they now protrude from the expanse of agitated water like the skeletons of some extinct sea-monsters of an earlier world. I liked especially to make my way to one of these isolated rocks, which is connected with the shore by a long iron bridge. To lean upon that parapet on a breezy day is almost as exhilarating as standing at the bow of a fine yacht in a stiff breeze, and has the advantage of involving no danger and discomfort. After a storm, the grandeur of the Atlantic at this point is almost indescribable; but even in comparatively calm weather the scene here is enchanting. At such a time the great variety of colors in the Bay of Biscay seemed to me unequaled. Far off, the sea is usually of the deepest blue, but nearer, is transformed into distinctly graduated shades of purple, lighter blue, and green, till finally it curls into successive lines of snow-white breakers, which chase each other up the cliffs as nimbly

and audaciously as charging squadrons of light cavalry. Delightful also is the contrast between the fury of the billows
on the tortured rocks, and the tranquillity which reigns in
sheltered nooks behind them, where only tender wavelets are
discernible—their soft, caressing fingers running along the sand
and ruffling it into letters whose meaning no man knows.
Meantime, everywhere and dominating all else is the ocean's
voice, now rising to a thunder of defiance, now sinking to a
soft entreaty or
a m u r m u r o f
delight; on one
side giving an
exultant shout
of victory, and
on the other a
soft whisper
of submission.
How typical of
the passions of
humanity are
these restless
waves,—tossed
on the bosom
of the sleepless

ROCKS AT BIARRITZ.

bay, in strict obedience to a power they cannot control, buf-
feted rudely by each other, driven by winds which make of
them their sport, and alternating ceaselessly between ferocity
and gentleness, war and peace, bewitching gaiety and solemn
majesty!

Behind the shattered rocks at Biarritz is a long, smooth
beach, curved like a crescent and paved with a hard floor of
sand. On this, as is usual in European seaside resorts,
stands the Casino, a rather showily painted and gilded edifice,
whose Moorish arches are, in the season, thronged with

Spanish, French, and English visitors, and resound to pleasing music. With the downfall of the Empire, however, the special glory of Biarritz departed, and it is hardly probable that it will ever again become the favorite resort of the *beau monde*, so famous during the reign of Napoleon III.

THE CASINO AND HOTELS AT BIARRITZ.

The Empress Eugénie (perhaps from its proximity to Spain, her native land) had a particular liking for this place, and regularly passed some portion of the summer here. In fact, the finest structure in Biarritz is the Villa Eugénie, built by Napoleon III to gratify his wife. I found it a sad object to visit. Once the abode of the most brilliant, fashionable court in Europe, it stands now separated from the town, as if abandoned to the sea. Its very isolation, which in the period of its glory gave to it distinction and exclusiveness, renders it now more desolate and dreary. I was not allowed to enter it, but through its barricaded windows I distinguished beautifully inlaid floors, mirrors and marble clocks, and handsome furniture which seemed awaiting the return of its owners to make them comfortable. Over the cornices of doors and windows I read the device: "N. E.," a melancholy reminder of the days when this was the seaside residence of the imperial household, and when the diplomats of Europe, as well as the highest dignitaries of France, paid homage here to the nephew of the great Emperor. To some extent, however, the formality of the Tuileries was laid aside here, and Biarritz was regarded by the Empress especially as a kind of neutral ground where she could meet with greater freedom her Spanish relatives and friends. Since my visit here, I understand that this imperial estate has been sold by Eugénie to a syndicate for one hundred thousand dollars, and will probably be converted into a hotel or casino. Curiously enough, the purchasers are obliged, by a clause in the deed of sale, to have masses celebrated every year in the churches of Biarritz on the anniversaries of the deaths of Napoleon III and the Prince Imperial.

CASINO AND THE VILLA EUGÉNIE.

In strolling on the sands between this villa and the town which it largely called into existence, one finds abundant food for thought. One hundred years ago, France entered on a marvelous cycle, which seems now completed. At the beginning, as at the end, of this eventful century, we see a French Republic. And yet between them how immense the contrast, how blood-stained are the intervening

steps! Through all the chaos of the Revolution, which swept
away the throne of Marie Antoinette; amidst the gory execu-
tions of the Reign of Terror; over the dazzling heights of Austerlitz and Wagram, and through the bloody depths of Waterloo

PAU.

and Sedan, poor France has moved heroically on, now dazed
with glory — now dumb with fear. To forty years of this
strange history has been affixed the letter "N." One half
of these have centred round the first Napoleon, the rest
around Napoleon III. One was colossal and heroic; the
other, by comparison, insignificant and weak. The voice of
one was a clarion call to victory; that of the other an imper-
fect echo. One was a Cæsar, born to rule; the other an
Augustulus, last of the Roman Emperors, who, if he wore for
a time the imperial robe, did so because that mantle once
adorned the man who perished, like Prometheus, on the sea-
girt rock of St. Helena.

One lovely day in spring, a short and picturesque railway
journey conducted us from Biarritz to Pau,—the best known

portal to the Pyrenees. We had already seen a number of
these mountains looming up on the horizon, for the huge
barrier wall dividing France from Spain, extends from the
surges of the Bay of Biscay to the classic waters of the Mediterranean; but it was only at Pau that we began to appreciate their grandeur and extent. Pau is to the Pyrenees what
Berne is to the Bernese Oberland, or Molde to the mountains
near the Romsdal. When I stepped out upon the balcony of
one of Pau's palatial hotels, and saw, directly opposite, and
seventy miles in length, a glorious panorama of sharp-cut,
snowy peaks, I felt as if I were looking on a glorious mosaic
of silver, set in a frame of lapis lazuli. If I am to be in the
presence of mountains for any length of time, I prefer looking at them from a distance, to seeing them close at hand.
For when their towering cliffs shut out the sunshine from
the valley,
and their stu-
pendous areas
of rock and
ice enclose
me like huge
prison walls,
I feel a stifling
sensation, and
long to gaze
upon them
from a stand-
point nearer
to the outside
world, where

VIEW FROM THE TERRACE AT PAU.

they can no more crush my spirits by their magnitude nor
fetter my imagination by their terrible reality. In this respect the view from Pau, while stimulating and inspiring, is
thoroughly restful and enjoyable. It is true, the names of

the principal summits in this silvery chain are not familiar to us, as are those of Switzerland, but their acquaintance is soon formed, and presently the Pic du Midi, the Vignemale, and the Maladetta become as well known as Mont Blanc, the Rigi, and the Matterhorn.

THE CASTLE AT PAU, FROM THE PARK.

These mountains form, however, only a dazzling background to the panorama visible from the promenade at Pau; for in the immediate foreground, fifty feet below the parapet on which we leaned, rushes the impetuous river Gave, the murmur of whose hurrying waters is distinctly heard; and between this and the white peaks themselves, still twenty miles away, are verdant plains and rolling wooded hills, dotted with villas, villages, and farms.

Although considered a health-resort, Pau's list of invalids is not so long as to depress the pleasure-loving tourist. Yet it is thought to have an ideal climate,—a trifle cold in winter, perhaps, but equable, and favored by a southern exposure and a cloudless sky. Those people, too (and there are not a few of them), who think that fierce winds are the emissaries of Satan sent to buffet them, and are driven well-nigh mad by the nervous irritability thus engendered, can find in Pau a place where strong winds are entirely unknown. During "the season," therefore, about four thousand visitors come

IN THE PARK AT PAU.

here annually. Unlike most sanitariums, however, Pau boasts of an eventful history. Its reason for existence does not lie in the exhilarating tonic of its mountain air or the enchanting scenery that it commands. For seven hundred years it was the capital of the old province of Béarn, renowned as one of the last strongholds of mediæval chivalry, and which became a part of France no longer ago than 1620. So independent was the spirit of its rulers, that one of them, when reproved because he had not taken part in the war between France and England, haughtily replied: "The wars between

England and France in no way concern me, for I hold my country of Béarn from God, by my sword, and by inheritance. There is, therefore, no reason why I should enter the service or incur the hatred of either of these kings.'' The old time-honored castle of the town is admirably preserved and is an object of the greatest veneration, not only as a fine memorial of former grandeur, but, in particular, as the birth-place and residence of the beloved Henry IV.

STATUE OF HENRY IV, PAU.

The gallant Henry of Navarre is still the idol of the Béarnese, and everything pertaining to his memory is as carefully cherished here as are souvenirs of Napoleon at the Hôtel des Invalides. There are several statues of him in the little town, the finest being the work of the sculptor, Raggi, in the Place Royale. This figure, which is more than life-size and of white marble, represents the "Good King" standing, with his right hand extended as if welcoming a friend, while the left rests easily on the hilt of his sword. Over his shoulder falls the long scarf that he often wore; and his well-known hat, with the traditional white plumes of Navarre, lies as if carelessly dropped, at his feet. Upon the pedestal are reliefs by Étex portraying scenes from Henry's childhood in these mountains, as well as some of his conspicuous deeds as king and warrior. Within the castle also, we found in almost every room, glowing upon canvas or woven in tapestry, the genial features of this sovereign. In studying his face I could readily believe the statement that he was noted not only for his bravery, but for his graceful manners,

THE TORTOISE-SHELL CRADLE OF HENRY IV.

fascinating conversation, and sprightly wit.   He was, in fact,
the incarnation of the happy, reckless, generous, pleasure-
loving spirit of that age.   Quick at repartee, fond of a jest,
at home on horseback or in camp, fearless in fighting, but not
vindictive, fond of the ladies, and devoted to his friends, it
is not strange
that the peo-
ple of his time
adored him, and
that his mem-
ory is cherished
still. Faults he
assuredly had,
but they were
the faults most
easily forgiven,
—those of the
heart. The best-
loved sover-
eigns of the
world have al-
ways been those
whose warm
impulses rather
than cold calcu-
lations have led
them into error.

HENRY IV.

Naturally the most interesting room in the castle is that
in which, on the 13th of December, 1553, the future Henry
IV first saw the light.   Suspended here, like the scale of a
balance, before a piece of fine old tapestry, is a large tortoise-
shell in which the royal infant is said to have been rocked.
It is true, in 1792, a revolutionary mob attempted to destroy
it, but it is now considered certain that the real cradle was

shrewdly preserved through the substitution of a false one in its place, which was indeed broken and burned with every insult.   Tradition asserts that when the child was born, his courageous mother, Jeanne d'Albret, sang an old Béarnese song, thus winning a wager from her father, the King of Navarre; and that the aged sovereign was so delighted at the advent of a boy, that he carried the infant in his arms, rubbed its lips with garlic, and even moistened its mouth with a few drops of the best Pyrenean wine.   At all events, the child grew up to be a lusty lad, for his grandfather, reproaching his daughter and son-in-law with having lost several children through French luxury, retained him in these mountains, and let him run bareheaded and barefooted with the children of the peasantry.   As a result, Henry arrived at manhood, manly and democratic in spirit and with a constitution of iron.   At the age of sixteen he led in battle his first cavalry charge, and at nineteen became King of Navarre.

THE CASTLE AT PAU.

Owing perhaps to this early training Henry, to the end of his life, never lost his sense of comradeship with the common people.   "I want my poorest subject," he said, "to have a fowl for his pot on Sundays."   Accordingly his people used to say of him: "He wears a heart as well as a crown."

It is said that on the day that Henry was assassinated in Paris by Ravaillac, a fearful tempest broke over this peaceful valley, and that the lightning struck the castle twice and shivered into atoms the King's initials carved upon the gate. What a misfortune that Henry's ashes do not rest, like those of Napoleon, beside his favorite river and among the people he loved so well! But the *sansculottes* of the Revolution made no discrimination between their kings; and Henry's body, like the rest, was rudely taken from the royal vault of St. Denis, and thrown into the ditch.

HOTEL GASSION AT PAU.

The souvenirs of Henry IV naturally cast into obscurity the other memories of this château. Yet two hundred years before his time a famous character of the Middle Ages made this place his home,—Gaston Phœbus, sovereign of Béarn and the adjoining county of Foix. Such was his fondness for the chase that he is said to have kept no less than 1,600 hounds, and Froissart, in his Chronicles, says of him: "Although I have seen very many knights, kings, princes, and others, I have never seen any so handsome, either in the form of his limbs, or in countenance, which was fair and ruddy, with gray, amorous eyes, that gave delight whenever he chose to express affection." At the same time he states that though Gaston "reigned prudently and was constant in his devotions," he never spared those who offended him, but ordered them to be thrown over the

walls or immured in dungeons.   He is even said to have killed
his own son in a fit of rage and to have tortured fifteen persons
whom he suspected of being his son's accomplices.   Strange
as it seems to us, no doubt this singular combination of manly

IN THE PYRENEES.

grace, ability, and devotion
with cruelty, lust, and ferocity presents a truthful picture of that age.   It was
in this castle also that the
Arab chieftain, Abd-el-Kader, was imprisoned for five
years.   He had defended
Algeria against the French
with wonderful ability, but
was compelled in 1847 to
yield to the overwhelming
forces of the enemy, and
was conveyed to France as
a prisoner of war.   Here he
remained till 1852, when he
was released by Louis Na-
poleon.   Five of his children died here in exile,
and Arabic inscriptions mark their graves.

It was with the most pleasurable anticipations that we
started out from Pau one beautiful June morning for the
mountains.   Certain we were, from even a distant view, that
we should thoroughly enjoy them.   Moreover, they had the
charm of being almost a *terra incognita*.

The Pyrenees are slighted by most European tourists.
Americans especially, who throng to far more inaccessible
parts of the Old World, seldom include these noble mountains
in their tour.   The reason must either be that they are not
fashionable or that their beauties are unknown.   It cannot be

for lack of scenery that the traveler does not go there; for
many of the Pyrenean peaks are worthy rivals of the Alps,
and Pyrenean valleys, as a rule, on account of their richer
southern vegetation, are lovelier than those of Switzerland.
Nor is it that the slightest hardship or discomfort is involved
in thoroughly exploring them.   There are no better roadways
in the world than those which France has made along this
barrier wall of France and Spain; and many Pyrenean hotels,
in furnishings, *cuisine*, and comfort, are worthy of comparison

ABD-EL-KADER AND NAPOLEON III.

with the best in Paris, from which indeed they are but fourteen hours distant.   The fact remains, however, that Switzerland is still the playground of the world, while southern
France receives comparatively few American and German,

and an inconsiderable number of English tourists. Even the travelers who go from France to Spain are usually satisfied with a distant view of the Franco-Spanish mountains, as they pass around them along the seacoast. Undoubtedly if the traveler were obliged to choose inexorably between the coun-

OBSERVATORY ON THE PIC DU MIDI.

try dominated by Mont Blanc and that surmounted by the Maladetta, he would better see the former; but after one or two visits to the land of William Tell, rather than to continue going thither, why should he not for a novelty enjoy an exploration of the Pyrenees? From Pau the railway runs almost parallel to the mountain chain, and at right angles to the numerous valleys which descend northward from it into France.   To understand the peculiar conformation of this region, one should compare the mountain range itself to the backbone of some huge skeleton, the ribs of which would correspond to the long parallel ridges projecting from it, while the intercostal spaces would be represented by the valleys thus divided from each other.   Into these narrow valleys, each of which has its rushing mountain stream, as well as scenic features distinctively its own, the Pyrenean tourist may ride in a comfortable carriage and over roads as perfectly macadamized and graded as the best in Switzerland. We found the air, however, so invigorating that

THE HERMIT OF THE OBSERVATORY.

we could not remain in the vehicle long at a time, but took delight in walking on, far in advance of the horses, and climbing here and there the wooded cliffs to see some waterfall whose music wooed us from the beaten path or to obtain some view denied us in the deep ravine. The first of these valleys which we explored contains, at a distance of about three miles from the entrance, the bathing establishment of Eaux Chaudes.

As we approached it, the scenery became imposing; the space between the mountains, which rose almost perpendicularly fifteen hundred feet above our heads, being hardly wide

enough for the driveway and the foaming torrent.   In fact,
the road is for the most part cut in the rock itself, frequently
hundreds of feet above the river, the roar of whose imprisoned waters echoing from the mountain walls made conversation here almost impossible.   At length, a sudden turn

THE GORGE OF EAUX CHAUDES.

revealed to us, wedged in between two precipices of great
height, the little hamlet of Eaux Chaudes.   Its form, like
that of New York (to compare small things with great),
is extremely long and narrow, for the reason that it has
been able to grow in only one direction.   Apart from a few
houses, one or two shops, and a small church, Eaux Chaudes

has only two conspicuous buildings. One is the bathing establishment; the other a plain, but scrupulously neat hotel, beneath whose balconies the river chafes and roars, as if enraged at the intrusion here of strangers. Two famous watering-places in the Pyrenees are here in close proximity, and are called respectively Eaux Chaudes and Eaux Bonnes. However, notwithstanding their descriptive names, the waters of the former are but very little warmer than those of the latter; nor are the springs of Eaux Bonnes "good" above all others in the Pyrenees. They lie in separate, though adjacent valleys, and the resorts themselves are of a widely different character. Eaux Chaudes is smaller and

THE BATHING ESTABLISHMENT AT EAUX CHAUDES.

less fashionable than its rival, and although many tourists select this as a starting-point for several notable excursions, the most of those who linger in this valley are invalids, who drink the water and take the baths because their health demands it. Still, we were well repaid for coming here, if only for the scenery. Moreover, here, as everywhere among the Pyrenees, we found the *cuisine* at the hotel excellent. "French cooking" is never better appreciated than in these mountain gorges, where one would naturally look for hardships and a meagre fare.

However, the linguistic powers of our landlord at Eaux Chaudes were not so perfect as his culinary skill.   In my room was a placard bearing a notice in several languages. The following was the English version:

EAUX CHAUDES.

" Daily's breakfast in apartment, five francs:
Daily's dinner at table d'hôte, five francs:
Conformably the tariff all meal taked out of the table
      d'hôte shall be paid one franc more for each meal:
One watch-lights, fifty centimes;
One sitting bath, seventy-five centimes:
The proprietor shall't be responsible for precious
      things unless they have deposit in the cash office:
Travelers without luggages are requested to pay
      every day."

Leaving Eaux Chaudes, and entering another of the gla-
cier-chiseled grooves which slope from the great Pyrenean
chain, we found ourselves upon a no less perfect road, than
that by which we had approached the hot springs.   By this,

only a few hours
after leaving
the first halting
place, we drove
into the village
of Eaux Bonnes.
This is a tiny bit
of Paris hidden
away among
the mountains,
twenty-five
hundred feet
above the sea.

AT EAUX BONNES.

Its entire area is only about half an acre, and so extremely
narrow is the gorge in which it lies, that it consists of only
two streets and an intervening park, so small, that to perceive
its band-stand and its little fountain at the same time, we
were obliged to step from its triangular enclosure into the

THE PARK AT EAUX BONNES.

street. Yet even in these straitened circumstances, Eaux Bonnes contains some thirty hotels and *pensions*, ranged in two lines on opposite sides of the park, and in such tantalizing proximity, that in dull times all the proprietors stand at their doors and stare each other out of countenance, or in the "season" calculate to a *sou* the profits of their rivals. Behind these buildings are precipitous cliffs, which have been

blasted away to give more space to the hotels. Only the front rooms, therefore, are available for tourists, since the sepulchral chambers in the rear, situated only two feet from the precipice, would be attractive merely to geologists. There are worse occu-

A STREET IN EAUX BONNES.

pations than sitting on the balcony of one of these hotels upon a pleasant evening and listening to the music in the illuminated park. One feels at such a time as if he were in the proscenium box of a diminutive theatre, listening to light opera.

The springs of Eaux Bonnes are considered wonderfully beneficial for pulmonary and spinal complaints; but as our lungs were sound and our backbones unyielding, we did not try the waters. Moreover, there was little inducement to do so, when we read the statement: "Evil consequences have arisen from a stranger's taking even a glassful to taste; and it is usual to begin with a tablespoonful and a half." However, one should not, for a moment, imagine that the attractions of Eaux Bonnes are limited by its ex-

EAUX BONNES AND THE PIC DE GER.

tremely circumscribed area. Numerous "promenades" have been laid out in the adjoining forests, leading to waterfalls or charming points of view, and these, when not made hori-

A CASCADE NEAR EAUX BONNES.

zontal, wind up the wooded cliffs in easy curves. For those who find even such ascents too difficult, a singular little donkey carriage is provided, which bears the comical name of *vinaigrette*. These tiny vehicles hold but one

A PYRENEAN VALLEY.

person, and in that respect suggest the cariole of Norway. The Pyrenean chaise is, however, as much more diminutive than the cariole, as the donkey is smaller than a Norwegian pony. Nevertheless, ridiculous as they at first appear, the tourist in the Pyrenees soon learns to like these *vinaigrettes*, and often hires them to attend him on his walks, that he may use them if he feels fatigued.

Of larger equipages, too, there is no lack here (though where the owners manage to store them is a mystery), and drives in the vicinity are varied and delightful. The glorious feature of Eaux Bonnes is, however, the famous Pic de Ger, more than

A PYRENEAN ROAD.

eight thousand feet in height, whose lordly summit forms the
background of the place, and in the glow of sunset towers
above the darkened village like the funeral pyre of some old
Scandinavian demigod.

In order to go from one Pyrenean valley to its parallel
neighbor, it is not always necessary to drive down to the plain,
and having, as it were, "doubled the cape," ascend the next
great mountain gorge; for some of the dividing ridges can

THE BRIDGE BUILT
BY NAPOLEON III
AT ST. SAUVEUR.

be crossed in carriages by a magnificent road, fully a hundred miles in length, constructed by Napoleon III. The reign of Louis Napoleon, however disastrous its ending, was not without much practical benefit to France. Not only did he make Paris the most beautiful city in the world; but here, five hundred miles away from it, along the southern boundary of his empire, he accomplished marvels in opening up and rendering accessible to travelers the Alps of France. The people of the Pyrenees are, therefore, grateful to him, and well they may be, since he contributed so much to their prosperity.

Again and again upon these drives we grew enthusiastic in our admiration of the splendid roads on which our carriage rolled, protected by stout parapets, upheld by arches, sheltered by tunnels, carried across deep chasms by enormous viaducts, constructed serpent-like along the face of cliffs which to the unprofessional traveler would seem impassable, and yet so gradually sloped that horses can ascend on them to altitudes of several thousand feet without undue fatigue, and trot with safety down the steepest mountain side.

One of the most conspicuous works accomplished here by Napoleon III is the marble bridge at St. Sauveur, of which indeed he laid the first stone in 1860. This splendid

A BIT OF PYRENEAN SCENERY.

specimen of engineering skill connects the opposite sides of a ravine in one great arch, and with a span of one hundred and fifty feet. Two hundred and eighteen feet below it the river seems to dwindle to a silver thread.

Viewed from some points along the valley, the bridge of Napoleon, as it is called, is the most picturesque structure of its kind that I have ever seen, its pure white marble standing out in beautiful relief against the sky, while through its curving frame the picture of dark forests and imposing mountains is a sight to linger evermore in the memory. The last time I beheld it was at sunset, when we had stopped our carriage to look back upon it, captivated by its loveliness. Beyond, a soli-

ONE OF THE PYRENEES.

tary mountain summit gleamed resplendent in the sunset glow; above it, several tiny pink and white clouds looked like soft rose petals lightly blown across the evening sky; the marble arch itself, a miracle of grace and beauty, seemed like a silver crescent, suspended from the velvety blue dome of heaven. One moment, as the rays of the declining sun fell full upon it, the spotless structure flushed like a mighty opal,—

"A rose of fire, shut in a veil of snow;"

then suddenly its glory vanished; the arch turned white and cold, and seemed the phantom of a bridge, rather than solid stone.   Reluctantly we drove on down the valley, realizing, with a sigh, that the sands of another happy day had ·ebbed away.

Another Pyrenean drive of perfect comfort, although conducted through a narrow gorge whose savage grandeur equals that of portions of the Alpine Via Mala, brought us one day to Cauterets, more than three thousand feet above the sea. In spite of its altitude and isolation from the outer world, we found this more of a town than any we had seen within the limits of the mountains.   Two hundred and fifty houses and some thirteen hundred permanent inhabitants give to this place, which Nature made so difficult of access, quite an urban air.   I liked it less, however, on this account.   The quiet of Eaux Bonnes was recollected with a sigh of regret, when, rising from the paved streets of this little town there came to us a constant din of rattling car-riages, crack-ing whips, and horses' hoofs, together with the clatter of wooden shoes and a contin-ual murmur of voices; for, in

CAUTERETS.

the limited area in front of the hotels (which, by the way, are admirable), guides, coachmen, servants, peasants, itinerant merchants, and scores of tourists seemed to be coming and going, expostulating, quarreling, bargaining, or gossiping at every hour of the day and night

Like almost all the other notable resorts within the shadow of the Pyrenees, Cauterets owes its existence and prosperity to its healing waters. In fact, these baths have always been more popular than those of Eaux Bonnes or Eaux Chaudes. French royalty has been frequently represented here, and one of the springs at Cauterets is said to have been visited by Julius Cæsar, and now bears his name. At all events, that the old Roman conquerors of Gaul and Spain knew of these waters and their healing proper- ties seems to be beyond ques- tion. With these

THE PIC DU MIDI.

advantages, the bathing establishment at Cauterets is, as we might expect, unusually fine. It is a marble structure, hand- some without and luxurious within,—containing white-tiled bath-rooms and two spacious apartments for swimming. Above these, a broad marble stairway leads to reading and billiard rooms, a café, a restaurant, and a small theatre. The use of these waters is, however, a serious affair, to be directed only by the resident physicians. The latest scientific appli- ances are employed, and one can be treated here in almost every conceivable way, from spraying to steaming, and from showering to soaking. For those who are not invalids, how- ever, the chief inducement for a visit to Cauterets is the

number of excursions to be made from it.   The most enjoyable of these I found to be the expedition to the Lac de
Gaube, a journey of about three hours on foot or horseback.
We started early in the morning, and the exhilarating ride up
a wild crevice in the mountains, flanked now by granite preci-

AT THE SNOW-LINE.

pices, now by huge black fir-trees, forms one of my most
delightful recollections of the Pyrenees.   At intervals halts
were made beside the waterfalls which, here as elsewhere in
these wooded mountains, are both numerous and beautiful.
The Lac de Gaube, the ultimate object of the excursion, is
one of the loneliest sheets of water in the world.   Nearly

six thousand feet above the sea, it lies in lofty isolation for almost the entire year, and even in the "season" is rarely seen by tourists. Yet it abundantly repays a visit, for, aside from its own beauty, above this lake, whose waters are of an exquisite green color, rises the famous Vignemale, one of the highest peaks of the Pyrenees, its sides and summit dazzling with eternal snow. Once, on visiting this place, we saw,

ON THE ROAD TO THE LAC DE GAUBE.

standing upon an isolated rock, a solitary man, whose meagre silhouette outlined itself against the sky, like an exclamation-point of wretchedness. Our guide, who told us he was the keeper of a little restaurant here, called to him several times without securing a response. Presently, however, he turned and came slowly toward us.

"Well," exclaimed our guide cheerfully, "how is business?"

"Business?" echoed the inn-keeper; "business? There

A PYRENEAN WATERFALL.

is no business! Look at my two boats there. I can't let them. Nobody will go out on the lake now. *Ces sacrés Anglais* have ruined me forever!"

We naturally inquired what "those cursed English" had done to injure him. In reply, he pointed out to us a little monument of white marble, surrounded by an iron railing. Approaching it, I read the following inscription:

"This tablet is dedicated to the memory of William Henry Pattison, of Lincoln's Inn, London, Esq., barrister-at-law; and of Susan Frances, his wife; who in the thirty-first and twenty-sixth years of their age, and within one month of their marriage, to the inexpressible grief of their surviving relatives and

THE LAC DE GAUBE.

friends, were accidentally drowned together in this lake, on the 20th day of September, 1832. Their remains were conveyed to England, and interred there at Witham, in the County of Essex."

"You see," exclaimed the boat-owner, when we had finished reading this, "I might as well drown myself, too, for all the money I make here!"

A PYRENEAN GIANT.

But," I replied, "this accident happened more than fifty years ago."

"What difference does that make," he retorted dismally, "since the monument is always here to keep it fresh in everybody's mind? People come here, just as you do, and they read that inscription. Monsieur says to Madame, 'Will you go out upon the lake?' and she says 'No, never, never!' and they go away and my boats are not let.   Is it not so?   *Mille tonnerres!*   Could not that Englishman have drowned his wife somewhere else than in my lake?   *Quel malheur!   Quel malheur!*"

The lamentations of this Jeremiah of the Pyrenees so touched our hearts that we embarked upon the lake of ill-

A PYRENEAN "PORT."

repute and gained some charming views which we should have completely missed had we remained on shore.   On our return, a luncheon of lake trout awaited us, and as we subsequently rode away, the lonely landlord chinked our silver pieces in his left hand, doffed his cap with his right, and cried: "*Merci, messieurs!*   If all the tourists were like you,

I might hope to recover some day from the injury done me by *ces sacrés Anglais.*"

It was from Cauterets that, on my second visit to the Pyrenees, I crossed the mountains into Spain as far as the baths of Panticosa. The route is the most

THE LAKE AT PANTICOSA.

difficult I ever traversed on a mule, save the descent into the Grand Cañon in Arizona. In fact, in many places it is

PART OF THE BARRIER WALL BETWEEN FRANCE AND SPAIN.

dangerous to ascend the barren cliffs in any way save on foot. Nevertheless the view toward Spain, as one comes through the rugged pass at a height of nearly nine thousand feet above the sea, gives ample compensation for the fatigue

AT PANTICOSA.

involved. Unlike the passage at the Port de Vénasque, which I shall presently describe, the Pyrenean crest-line at this point is almost as sharp as the ridge-pole of a house. We stepped over it, as across a threshold, and stood for a moment with one foot in France and the other in Spain. I think I was never more tired in my life than when I approached Panticosa. I had been assured by my guide that it was a trip of only eight hours from Cauterets, but it was fully twelve hours after we had mounted our saddles at the Pyrenean watering-place before we reached our destination. As we made our

THE BATHS OF PANTICOSA.

way with painful slowness down the mountain side, I saw
below me a perfectly treeless basin in the midst of desolate
granite cliffs, some of which rose to a great perpendicular
height, reminding me of the precipices of the Gemmi above
Leuk in Switzerland. The centre of this area was occupied
by a small lake which looked as cold and lifeless as that of

IN THE BATHS OF PANTICOSA.

the great St. Bernard. Around this, however, were several
buildings, which proved to be the bathing establishment,
hotels, and boarding-houses. In these about six hundred
guests can be accommodated, and in the "season" the place
is said to be crowded to its utmost capacity. Unfortunately,
I visited Panticosa before the influx of any such multitude,
and the only visitors here were a few saffron-colored Spaniards
with their wives, who seemed to be bored to death, and envied
me apparently my speedy return to France. The titles of
the baths at Panticosa amused me greatly. Instead of

being dedicated, as in France, to some divinity or patron saint, they have been frankly named after the parts of the body they are supposed to cure. Thus over one door I read the words: "The Stomach;" over another, "The Lungs;" a third was called "The Liver;" a fourth "The Purger;" and finally one, that sent a cold chill down my spine, bore the significant legend,—"The Colic."

I shall never forget being ushered by an attendant into one room at Panticosa, the sulphurous odor from which was so extremely pungent that, when the door opened, it seemed to me that a box of lucifer matches had been ignited and was being held beneath my nose. The room was partially filled with steam, and in the obscurity I beheld, to my great

"THE CHAOS."

astonishment, a perfectly naked man leaping madly about, as
if he were an insane patient dancing the " Highland Fling,"
while an attendant was playing on him through a hose some
almost scalding sulphur-water. At every jump the wretched
man gave utterance to a howl of pain, and turned about like
a spinning top in his anxiety to offer some cooler surface of
his body to the heated stream. Finally, with a wild roar,

as though his
limit of endur-
ance had been
passed, he start-
ed, bounding
and shrieking,
towards the
door where I
was standing. I
turned and fled,
as if the sul-
phurous fiend
himself were
after me, and
did not stop
until I reached
the outer steps
of the establish-

ON THE WAY TO PANTICOSA.

ment. Even then I was obliged to cough, sneeze, and
strangle for some minutes before I could expel the fumes of
sulphur from my head and throat; and now, though several
years have passed since then, if I partake of Welsh rabbit
late at night, I sometimes see, in troubled dreams, not the
traditional features of "my grandmother," but the appalling
figure of that parboiled wretch of Panticosa, leaping and
roaring as if possessed of devils and executing antics any one
of which could have been justly called a sulphur spring.

Of all the excursions that I made within the limits of the Pyrenees none stands out in my memory with greater vividness than that which led me to the amphitheatre of Gavarnie.

THE AMPHITHEATRE OF GAVARNIE.

There are indeed few objects in the world which have impressed me more. The savage grandeur of the route approaching it prepares one in a measure for the final scene of desolation and sublimity. For a considerable distance the road winds thither through a labyrinth of monstrous rocks, known as the Chaos. Except in Norway I have never seen boulders, at once so numerous and gigantic, as these moss-covered remnants of disintegrated mountains, hundreds of which are larger than an ordinary church. One shudders to imagine the convulsion that took place here when whole cliffs, driven by an earthquake shock, were toppled over into this ravine, and, rushing down from either side like two opposing troops of cavalry, met with a shock that shattered them to fragments. Many in horrible confusion mounted high upon their fellows, grinding the ones below into the soil of the valley in which they still lie half imbedded; others were split by the encounter into an inconceivable variety of distorted shapes; while others still, too large to break or to recoil, lie front to front, unyielding and immovable. The awful roar of that appalling avalanche apparently sufficed for all time, for it has been succeeded by unbroken silence. Perhaps, in the course of ages, Nature may even cover the remains of these colossal combatants. A few miles distant from this gloomy Chaos is the amphitheatre of Gavarnie,—a semicircle of stupendous precipices at whose base the French Republic terminates and Spain begins. As has been said, the Pyrenean valleys extend north and south, like parallel grooves carved out by prehistoric glaciers, as they forced a passage from the mountains to the plain. These valleys usually end quite impercep-tibly, ascending gradually to the loftier regions; but the Gavar-nie cañon main-tains its level

A SECTION OF GAVARNIE.

fairly well, till, at its ultimate extremity, a curving wall of well-nigh perpendicular cliffs suddenly rises to a prodigious height. These cliffs are parts of three great mountains,

ranging from ten to eleven thousand feet in height, which
have united thus to form a triple alliance of stupendous precipices, secure against the invasion of the world. It was on an
afternoon in June that I stood, speechless, in this mighty cul-
de-sac. I felt as if I were a pygmy standing in the arena of
a Colosseum within which all the deities of mythology could
have found ample room. A bird flying in a straight line
from one side of this amphitheatre to the other would traverse the distance of a mile. The huge black walls are absolutely bare of vegetation. Their curving parapet, shaped like
the horseshoe archway of the Moors, is covered with eternal
snow, but on their almost vertical surfaces nothing can find
lodgment, save where on some projection a miniature glacier

GAVARNIE.

basks chame-
leon-like in the
bright sun, or
where the nu-
merous cas-
cades from up-
per snow-fields
pause for a sec-
ond in their sil-
very descent up-
on some ledge of
granite. One of
these falls ex-
ceeds in altitude
any cataract in
Europe, having
a height of thir-
teen hundred and eighty feet. Its volume, it is true, is quite
diminutive, and, like the Staubbach, it is dissipated into
spray before it reaches the arena; and yet it is this small
adventurous stream that gives birth to the river Gave, which

subsequently rushes musically by the promenade at Pau. Cascades are not, however, the only contributions that the snow-capped mountains make to this arena; for, standing here, we heard at frequent intervals a sullen roar like distant thunder, and could perceive, far up, upon the cliffs, a torrent of descending snow and ice, coursing through channels grooved by former avalanches through unnumbered centuries.

ROLAND'S CLEFT.

As we rode out of the arena of Gavarnic, we turned to see to better advantage the glittering summits that surmount it. In the level crest of one of them is a singular indentation, which at this distance appears no larger than a cavity made by the loss of a front tooth. Small as it looks, however, from the valley, this insignificant notch in the great mountain wall is more than nine thousand feet above the sea, and is a kind of rectangular window looking into Spain, three hundred feet in width and three hundred and fifty in height. This is the famous Cleft of Roland, to which attaches one of the most romantic legends of the Pyrenees. Thus tradition says that when Charlemagne, in 778, had finally rolled back from France the northward moving wave of Saracenic conquest, and was pursuing the Moors across the Pyrenees into Spain, he found the mountain wall above the

ON PYRENEAN HEIGHTS.

amphitheatre of Gavarnie utterly impassable. Riding beside him then, as usual, was the half-mythical hero of mediæval chivalry, Roland, whose courage, love affairs, and exploits were to form for centuries themes for romantic poetry. Charlemagne, therefore, called upon this famous paladin to open a passage for the army; and Roland, in response, with one tremendous stroke of his great sword, cut in the mountain's crest the opening still called Roland's Cleft, through which the invading army passed exultantly.

To one who journeys eastward, along the French side of the Pyrenees, the halting places steadily increase in interest and beauty, the climax being reached in the most

IN THE PARK OF LUCHON.

popular of all the Pyrenean resorts,—Luchon. This charming
spot reminded me of Baden-Baden, in its long shaded avenues, its fine ho-
tels, its tempt-
ing shops and
flower-stalls, its
mineral baths
and fountains,
and the variety
of walks and
drives which
make a lengthy
sojourn here de-
lightful. The
loveliness of Ba-

THE CASINO AT LUCHON.

den-Baden's Lichtenthaler Allée is here approximately reproduced in an extensive park with well-kept lawns, fine trees,
an artificial lake with swans, and rustic summer-houses where
we passed many pleasant hours listening to music, watching
the promenaders, and looking off on the enchanting scenery
surrounding us. Nor was there lack of amusement here when
darkness veiled
the mountains
from our sight,
for Luchon has
a fine casino
with restaurant
and reading-
room, concert-
hall, and thea-
tre where opera
is given every

THE THERMAL ESTABLISHMENT, LUCHON.

other night, and lesser entertainments are provided almost
daily. A stay of twenty-four hours in Luchon convinced us

it would have been a grave mistake to come here first, and thus reverse the order of the route. Eaux Bonnes and Cauterets, though pleasing in themselves, seemed to us tame in comparison. Luchon and its surroundings proved to be so delightful, that I could not forgive myself for having allowed so many summers to elapse without enjoying it.

> "Oh, the years I lost before I knew you, love!
> Oh, the hills I climbed and came not to you, love!
> Ah, who shall render unto us to make us glad
> The things which for and of each other's sake
> We might have had?"

The most enjoyable of all the numberless excursions to be made here is the trip to the Port de Vénasque, through which is seen the giant of the Pyrenees, the Maladetta.

NEAR LUCHON.

This "port" or notch in the mountain wall, somewhat resembling the Cleft of Roland, is only a few hours distant from Luchon, yet there are not a dozen excursions I have ever made in any portion of the world that I so cherish in my list of inspiring memories as the trip to that aërial gateway, eight thousand feet above the level of the sea. The Port de Vénasque (so called from a neighboring Spanish village of that name) is a natural doorway between France and Spain, and many are the merchants, mule-drivers, and tourists who pass through it annually. To

one who approaches it from the French side the view which
it reveals is an instantaneous revelation, for intervening rocks
conceal till the last moment all that lies beyond, and one
ascends to it as to a portal leading to some castle in the
clouds.   Never shall I forget the moment when turning a
sharp cliff I saw before me that gigantic fissure in the mountain crest, several hundred feet in height, yet only fourteen
feet in breadth.   It is thus a mere crack or loop-hole in
the Pyrenean battlements, hardly discernible from a distance.
Within its shadow is an iron cross, marking the boundary

ON THE WAY TO THE
PORT DE VÉNASQUE.

between the two countries, but this we could not linger to
examine, for a strong wind was sweeping through this narrow
aperture, and we were almost literally blown straight through
the " port " from France to Spain.   Sheltering ourselves,
however, on the southern side, we looked with bated breath
upon the scene before us.   Directly opposite, and separated
from us by an awful chasm, rose in stupendous majesty the
Maladetta, covered with everlasting snow save where some

THE MALADETTA.

sharp peaks pierced the ice-crust like gigantic tusks.   Its area
is enormous, and as my astonished gaze traveled along its
miles of glaciers glittering in the sun, and then descended to
the frightful gulf between us, which has for ages been the
desolate receptacle of all the Maladetta's avalanches, it seemed
to me the contrast was as striking and as sharply drawn as
between Paradise and the Inferno.   And yet, aside from the
display of its vast area of sunlit glaciers, I realized that this
monarch of the Pyrenees was terrible in its austerity.   Had
not the sun been turning all its snow-fields into a silvery

coat of mail, it would have justified its name of the "Accursed Mountain," for neither animal nor vegetable life can possibly exist upon its naked cliffs and icebound crest. For years it was regarded, like the Matterhorn in Switzerland,

THE PORT DE VÉNASQUE.

as fatal to the man who should attempt its conquest. Nor were such superstitious fears unfounded; for once, in trying to ascend it, a guide fell headlong into one of its crevasses in the presence of his son, and his body was never recovered. At last, however, in 1842, the conquest of the mountain was achieved, its summit being reached by five adventurous

NEAR THE PORT DE VÉNASQUE.

cragsmen after a struggle of four days and nights. A curious
legend is connected with the Maladetta. Peasants believe
that this now Arctic region was once a beautiful pasture-land,

covered with
grazing sheep.
Christ, it is said,
came to visit its
shepherds, but
was stoned by
them; where-
upon the moun-
tain was imme-
diately turned
to a mass of

A PYRENEAN BRIDGE.

rocks and ice, and all the men and animals upon its surface
perished.

My last view of the monarch of the Pyrenees, as I paused
for a moment before reëntering the Port de Vénasque, will
never be forgotten. The gulf of desolation at my feet was
dark with shadows. Even the granite precipices of the
"Accursed Mountain" had long since lost the rays of the declining sun. But all the icy summit of the Maladetta, miles
in length, displayed a constantly increasing wealth of splendor, as its white surface reddened with the sunset glow.
Spellbound, I watched the magic work of the departing god
of day, as he transmuted, silently but potently, each snow-
crest, pinnacle, and glacier from silver into gold. Meantime,
however, shadows were rising, demon-like, from out the yawn-
ing chasm to expel this heavenly visitor and justify the mountain's name. Up, up, they crept, scaling the giant buttresses
and icy slopes with ease, and driving steadily before them the
sun's glory, which in its gradual retreat abandoned first one,
and then another outpost, until the highest pinnacles alone
retained their lustre, like battlements of a celestial city. At

length, even these began to change,—assuming hues which can perhaps be named but not described. The glow of gold, the heart of a pale rose, the flush on the cheek of a sleeping child, and finally the soft gray on the breast of a dove,—this seemed to me the sequence of those waning shades. Then, when the entire mountain had turned white and cold, I watched the tiny cloud-fleets put forth from the headlands of the Maladetta and float away from their moorings into a sea of silvery blue. These, for a time, still caught the solar radiance on their snowy sails; but finally the moment came when even their colors disappeared, melting away into a dawn for other eyes than ours.

As Pau was the portal by which we entered the region of the Pyrenees, so the last place in which we lingered, ere we left these mountains on our journey eastward, was Lourdes. Beautiful for situation is this famous place of pilgrimage, nestling among the foothills of the Pyrenees at the junction of two mountain streams, and built around the base of a precipitous rock crowned by an ancient fortress. This castle of

LOURDES.

Lourdes has had a most eventful history, much of which is recorded in the chronicles of Froissart. Not all of its varied fortunes can be recounted here, but every traveler who looks upon its grim old battlements sees at a glance that once it must have commanded the entire valley, and in the wars of the Middle Ages was a citadel of great importance. Originally founded by the Romans, it was deemed impregnable be-

THE HOME OF BERNADETTE.

fore the invention of cannon, and is still strong enough to have served in its old age as a place of detention for some German prisoners during the Franco-Prussian war.

But the importance and prestige of this old stronghold have now been eclipsed by those of a beautiful Gothic church, which crowns another eminence, and, on account of its clear white stone resembling marble, is visible from a great distance. A stranger, knowing nothing of the history of Lourdes, would be astonished to discover such an imposing church as this in a small

THE GROTTO.

mountain town with only about six thousand inhabitants; but when he walks to a humble cottage here, and, starting from that point, investigates the wonderful influence exerted by the faith of a poor girl who lived here more than fifty years ago, its presence is no longer a mystery.

OUR LADY OF LOURDES.

The name of this peasant girl was Bernadette Soubirous. Her parents, like most of the villagers, were plain, hardworking people. One summer afternoon in 1858, the child, then fourteen years of age, went out as usual to gather wood. Suddenly, while passing a grotto by the side of the road, she is said to have heard a peculiar noise, and, looking into the cavern, to have beheld there a vision of the Holy Virgin clad in a long white robe and silvery veil, with a light blue sash, and slippers

adorned with golden roses. Among the words which she declared the Virgin addressed to her then and on subsequent
occasions were the following: "Go tell the priests to build a
church for me here." "Go drink, and wash in a fountain
that will miracu-
lously spring up
before you." In
response to Ber-
nadette's en-
treaties that she
would favor her
with her name,
the celestial vis-
itor replied, "I
am the Immac-
ulate Concep-
tion."

CANES AND CRUTCHES IN THE GROTTO.

Descending
to a point below
the church, and entering the grotto where these miraculous
manifestations are said to have occurred, I saw before me,
in a niche of the rock, a statue of the Virgin surmounted
by the words which she is said to have uttered: "I am the
Immaculate Conception." Near this, also, surrounded by a
marble coping, is the miraculous fountain which is said to
have gushed forth in obedience to the Virgin's command. I
never failed, in repeated visits, to see a crowd of people
kneeling before this and imploring the aid of Mary, while the
rock itself is garnished with hundreds of canes and crutches,
the thank-offerings of those who claim to have been cured by
the water. It was Sunday morning when I first approached
this grotto, and the place, which is always more or less full,
was then thronged with kneeling worshipers. The water of
this fountain has been chemically examined, but whatever

natural virtue it has, beyond that of simply pure water, is too subtle to be discovered. Nevertheless, during the summer of my visit, the number of pilgrims to Lourdes averaged fifty thousand per month, and, for the benefit of absentees, the healing waters are now sent forth to various parts of Europe, like those of the Apollinaris and Selzer springs. In summer special trains are run to Lourdes bringing thousands of invalids and pilgrims, together with many tourists who avail themselves of the cheap rates to make a visit to the Pyrenees. Zola, in his novel, "Lourdes," gives of these throngs of pilgrims some of the most graphic descriptions he has ever penned.

Above the grotto is the church which the priests built in obedience to the Virgin. It is in some respects the most singular sanctuary I ever saw. Turning my eyes toward the roof, one hundred feet above the kneeling worshipers who filled the nave, I could see nothing but a mass of variously colored silken banners suspended from the ceiling, as triumphant proofs of the reality of Bernadette's vision. Moreover, the chapels, and, in fact,

INTERIOR OF THE CHURCH AT LOURDES.

most of the walls of the church are covered with gilded hearts, medallions, and votive tablets of white marble—all testifying to miraculous cures effected by the sacred spring.

How history repeats itself in different ages and in various

lands! Votive tablets like these are nothing new. They have been found in ancient temples by the Ganges, amid the ruins of Carthage, and in the crumbling shrines of Heliopolis and Palmyra; and in every case the grateful donors thought they had been cured or saved by the different deities to whom their supplications were offered.

HOTEL KEEPER AT LOURDES.

From a practical point of view, the vision of Bernadette has proved a blessing to her townspeople. Almost every barber, shoemaker, and grocer here has a sign over his door, declaring that his shop is dedicated to the "Lady of Lourdes," and, near the grotto, are many shops and booths where all sorts of religious relics and trinkets are offered for sale. I am sorry to say, however, that the morality of the place is not of the first order. In one of these shops a lady of our party had her pocket picked, while in another a similar attempt was made upon my own. The relatives of Bernadette, who herself died in a convent many years ago, are the most fortunate of the villagers, for they turn their relationship to pecuniary profit. Thus, over the door of one shop I read, "This is the store of Bernadette's aunt;" over a second, "This is kept by a cousin of Bernadette;" while a third bore the seductive notice: "Here you may see the girl who was present with Bernadette at the third apparition."

So many thousands of pilgrims visit Lourdes every year that the hotels are flourishing. In one of them at table d'hôte I found two separate companies, each with a different menu; a meagre bill of fare being provided for the saints and a more elaborate one for the sinners. Candor compels me to acknowledge that, indifferent to my reputation for sanctity, I chose the table where I could get the best meal.

An eastern fable tells us that when Paradise was fading from the earth, a single rose was saved and treasured by an angel, who gives to every mortal, sooner or later, in his life, one breath of fragrance from the immortal flower,—one alone, but it is worth a million ordinary breaths.

There are some favored portions of our earth where one can easily persuade himself that he inhales this perfumed air of Paradise; and one of them surely is that stretch of beautifully curving coast, which has the Maritime Alps for an imposing background and the blue Mediterranean for a frontispiece, and is known as the Riviera.

This name, with its soft,

ON THE RIVIERA.

mellifluous vowels, has power to stimulate a multitude of joyful anticipations in those who have never visited this enchanting shore, and to evoke as many happy memories in those who have once lingered here. Screened from the

v. — 15

northern winds and basking in the sun, the Riviera is the first point where birds of passage, going southward, halt for the winter; and thousands of people from the north of Europe, now follow the example of these feathered songsters, and

A SUGGESTION OF THE ORIENT.

find a sunny, health - restoring winter residence within this earthly paradise.

Along the Riviera, between Nice and Genoa, stretches the finest coast-drive in the world, —the Cornice, which, as its name implies, is a mere shelf of rock between the mountains and the Mediterranean, following the numberless indentations of the shore, and often either absolutely cut out from the cliffs, or carried through them.

Like so many other famous roads in Europe, this was begun by Napoleon I, who needed it as a means of military communication between France and Italy; but now, as every one knows, a railway has been built in close proximity for those who wish to travel here more rapidly than in a carriage.

But who that has a heart responsive to the historic and beautiful will ever consent, unless necessity compels the sacrifice, to be whirled along through scenery like this, boxed up in a railway compartment, unable to gain a glimpse of much of his magnificent environment, and passing that which is discernible too hastily for adequate appreciation? In such a place the railway should be used merely to transport baggage, while the tourist himself is driven leisurely along a route which constantly reveals new beauties and surprising contrasts,— now skirting a long, wave-lapped beach, now sweeping inland with a curving bay, now passing groves of patriarchal olive-trees, or winding between walls half hidden under terraced vines, or glittering with the golden fruit of lemon-trees, or overrun with clambering roses, and yet again, at intervals, mounting high above the sea which breaks in jeweled foam against the base of overhanging cliffs.

Another tradition of this region says that Eve, as she was going forth from Eden, plucked a lemon from a tree beside the gate, and brought it with her into the outer world. Subsequently, in wandering about the earth, she threw the lemon down at Mentone, where it grew and multiplied; and thus it is that on the Riviera there is one thing that really came from Paradise.

Palm-trees are also numerous on the Riviera, and the village of Bordighera, which has for centuries supplied St. Peter's with its palms for Easter, is surrounded by vast numbers of them, some of which are said to be a thousand years old.

There is, therefore, along this Med-

A VILLA ON THE RIVIERA.

iterranean coast a faint suggestion of the Orient, not only in
the ardent sun which pours upon it such a flood of light and
heat, but in this tree of romance and of poetry, which hints
to us of eastern shores which the same ocean laves, where
palms have cast their shadows on the founders of Buddhism,
Christianity, and Islam, in the prolific Orient,— cradle of
religious faiths.

On one side are
the vine-clad, ol-
ive-mantled hills,

THE HARBOR OF NICE.

NICE.

dotted with ruined
towers, picturesque
castles and church-
es, sunburnt vil-
lages and pretty
villas perched like
eagle's nests upon
the mountain sides,
and on the other the illimitable sea, receding in unbroken
splendor till the horizon line is lost in sparkling light.

Occasionally, beyond the sapphire water and the wave-
worn rocks, one can discern from the Riviera the shadowy
profile of Corsica, the birthplace of that man, whose life
began and ended on an island, and whose eventful history is
bounded by the obscurity of Corsica, and the captivity of St.

Helena. At frequent intervals, the sea spreads out a lace-like net of creamy surf before some picturesque Italian village, where houses, churches, ruined towers, and convents rise tier above tier on the hillside, relieved against a wall of purple mountains and snow-covered peaks, and all magnificently dowered by the sun. It is true, much of the romance of these villages disappears on close inspection; but from a distance, especially at the hour of sunset, the impression they produce is indescribable, and the bells which then chime forth in liquid tones the Ave Maria, sound, I fancy, as sweetly as ever did the siren voices, which poets tell us used to echo over this same enchanting sea. At such a time

THE BAY OF ANGELS, NICE.

one can well understand why the luxurious Greeks and Romans formerly loved to linger on this shore, forgetting even the marble palaces of Rome and the blue skies of Baiæ and Surrentum.

Of all the pleasure-resorts along the Riviera Nice is the most frequented, since it has most to interest and amuse the winter resident.

Nice, is in fact, a city of nearly seventy thousand inhabitants, with hotels as expensive and luxurious as those of the largest European capitals, together with clubs, concert-halls, and an opera-house where have appeared many of the illustrious artists of the world. Its elegant promenades are, therefore, during the season, thronged with fashionable people, and life here for several months of the year is a perpetual round of pleasure. The climate of Nice, although colder in winter than in more sheltered portions of the Riviera, is usually called delightful, but those who come here thinking that winter is entirely unknown will make a serious mistake.

Sunshine and a mild southern atmosphere are, it is true, its prevailing characteristics; but there are days in Nice and Cannes, and even in the sheltered amphitheatre of Mentone, where cold winds are trying to the invalid; for one must not forget that north of the Riviera are mountains, some of which are covered for months with ice and snow. When, therefore, the wind blows southward from these reservoirs of frost, the effect is very perceptible, and might be unhealthful, were not the coast so thoroughly heated by the sun, which rolls its waves of warmth upon this sheltered region through a dry atmosphere and an almost cloudless sky. As a rule, however, the benefit of the climate of the Riviera is due to the fact that it is rarely cold and wet here at the same time. Thus, when a north wind blows it may be cold at Nice, but the air is dry; and when, on the other hand, the wind comes from the

A SHELTERED NOOK.

south and the temperature is mild, the air is moist. From observation in different countries and climates, it is my opinion that Americans, and northern tourists in general, make too little difference, when in the south of Europe, between sun and shade and between the middle of the day and the evening. The direct solar heat is such, that they forget to guard themselves from the much colder air of the unheated galleries and churches, and from the rapid lowering of temperature caused by the disappearance of the sun.

Moreover, accustomed as we are to warmer houses than foreigners gener-
ally possess, we often make the mistake of trying to accustom ourselves in Europe to chilly rooms, simply because the guests of other nationalities dispense with fires in

MONACO AND MONTE CARLO.

theirs. To be comfortable in winter anywhere in southern Europe, one not only needs rooms with a southern exposure, but should indulge freely in the luxury of open fires. This is true at times even in Cairo, where I have known an apartment without fire to be miserably uncomfortable in the mornings and evenings.

One of the loveliest portions of the Riviera, and, in fact, one of the most exquisitely beautiful features on the face of Mother Earth, is the principality of Monaco. It lies in the very heart of the Riviera like the gorgeous buckle of some outstretched belt. The Maritime Alps rise tier on tier behind it, while before it is the Mediterranean, stretching away to Africa, peerlessly blue at midday, and in the glow of sunset glittering with iridescent colors like a vast expanse of molten opals.

Strictly speaking, this principality is not a part of France, but it is surrounded by it on three sides, and is so much a part of Nice, which is on French soil only ten miles distant, that it may be regarded as a kind of annex to the French Republic.

The town of Monaco itself must have been in olden times an ideal fortress, for it is perched upon a huge flat rock advancing boldly into the sea, with well-nigh perpendicular cliffs nearly two hundred feet above the waves.

The Prince of Monaco in many respects resembles a king in comic opera. His principality covers only about eight square miles of territory, and his palace is an odd-looking building, strongly suggestive of mediæval times with its portcullises and drawbridges, yet hinting too of modern warfare with its pyramidal groups of cannon-balls.

Nevertheless, within this little territory this Prince is an absolute monarch, who makes his own laws, hires his own soldiers, issues his own postage-stamps and coinage, and possesses a small semi-military police force, and for a navy — his private yacht! He rejoices also in the title of "Albert I, Prince and Sovereign by the grace of God," and boasts of an ancestry dating back nearly a thousand years, for the Princes of Monaco are descendants of a noble family of Genoa. He even has his ministers at the Courts of Vienna, Madrid, Rome, and Paris. Unlike the rest of the world, the inhabitants of Monaco pay no taxes; for the principality is really governed by a Syndicate which makes all local improvements, defrays all the expenses of government, and pays the Prince a handsome annual allowance in return for the privilege of carrying on the famous gambling establishment of Monte Carlo.

The Casino, where the gambling goes on, is situated on a
bluff that overlooks the sea, and is surrounded by a series of
enchanting terraces and gardens, where one can seat himself
beneath the drooping fringes of the palms, or stand on marble
staircases, and look between exotic plants and over walls
adorned with a profusion of red roses, upon the loveliest
ocean in the world.   Yet even this unrivaled combination of
man's art and
Nature's prodi-
gality will not
suffice to keep
you from enter-
ing the Casino
here. There is
no charge for ad-
mission, though
you will prob-
ably contribute
something to
the Syndicate
before you get
out. Cross the
threshold, and a

THE CASINO AT MONTE CARLO.

servant in livery will greet you with a polite bow, as if you
were an expected guest, and will usher you into a hall where
several respectable looking gentlemen in dress suits scrutinize
you carefully, and, if satisfied with your appearance, will present you with a card of admission available for one day.
Your behavior will determine whether you may receive
another card, or not.   Leaving your hat and cane, for which
you receive a check, you stroll perhaps for a few minutes
through the building, if the hour for gambling has not arrived.   You will admire its construction and embellishment,
for it was designed by Charles Garnier, the architect of the

Grand Opera House in Paris, and you will find here not only a well-furnished reading-room, but a gorgeously decorated theatre, where twice a day an orchestra of eighty well-trained musicians gives a delightful concert.

A GAMBLING-HALL AT MONTE CARLO.

On entering the spacious gambling-halls, you will perceive a number of long tables, in the centre of each of which is a sunken bowl, containing a revolving wheel. This wheel has thirty-seven divisions, marked from zero upward, and alternating red and black, and when this is whirled from right to left, a little ball is thrown into it in the opposite direction. Finally, as both wheel and ball acquire a slower motion, the latter drops into one of the divisions, determining thus the lucky number, and also the successful color, either red or black. At each table are seated four men called *croupiers*, while a fifth man is also in attendance to overlook the game and settle disputes. Upon the green baize cloth are numbers, corresponding to the divisions in the wheel, and so arranged that one can bet on red or black, and odd or even, as well as on any special figure. The smallest bet on these roulette tables is five and the largest six thousand francs. Before starting the game, the *croupiers* notify the players to place their stakes, and just before the ball falls into a division, they forbid any more play with the well-known words: "*Le jeu est fait. Rien ne va plus.*" Then, at the conclusion of each play, they call out the winning number and color, and the men at the ends of the table with long rakes draw in the money which the bank has won, and also with wonderful celerity and skill pay out gold or silver or bank-notes to those who have been fortunate.

No one can watch these men for any length of time, without perceiving that the nervous strain they undergo is very great; and, as a matter of fact, they have to be relieved every two hours. Every day, Sunday included, from noon until midnight, these gambling-halls are crowded. Everything is quiet and orderly; no voice is heard above an undertone; and almost the only sounds

AT MONTE CARLO.

are the chink of the gold and silver coins, and the monotonous words of the croupiers. In fact, were it not for the intense suppressed excitement at these tables the place would be depressingly dull. Accordingly, one who cares nothing for the game, and who is not interested in studying the phases of humanity at the tables, soon gladly leaves the halls, either to walk about the lovely garden or to listen to one of the finest orchestras in Europe.

The only thing that can be said in favor of the gambling is that it is honestly conducted, no cheating being possible for either the bank or the players. Indeed, when any one has been exceptionally fortunate and has won a large sum of money, two or more guardians of the Casino usually accompany him to his hotel; for, several years ago, a foreigner was murdered here soon after leaving the gambling-hall, and since then the authorities have been on the alert to prevent the repetition of a crime which, by destroying public confidence, would do them an incalculable injury.

Until the introduction of electricity, oil lamps were preferred to gas in the Casino; for, some years since, a clever trick was played here by a band of rogues, one of whom turned off the gas at the meter, while his confederates took advantage of the darkness and confusion to grab whatever money was on the tables, and even to rob the players.

In some cases the authorities give a bankrupt player money enough to pay his fare home. This is, however, regarded as a loan, and must be paid before the recipient of the money can ever again enter the Casino. It is said that over two hundred thousand dollars are annually advanced in this way to gamblers who have been left utterly destitute.

The profits of this business must be enormous, for after subsidizing the Prince, relieving his subjects from taxation, and paying its own large staff of employees, from members of its famous orchestra to its croupiers and gardeners, the Syndicate is reputed to gain about one million, six hundred thousand dollars annually.

The bank of Monte Carlo always has a percentage in its

favor; but it makes its greatest gains because of the almost universal rule that if a man wins he will play on till he loses. A story is told of a man who in a few hours won here eighty thousand dollars. The croupier reported the loss to the proprietor, Monsieur Blanc, who only smiled, and sent a servant to the gentleman's hotel to see if he had gone. When he returned and reported that the man was still there, Monsieur Blanc laughed softly, and said: "*Très bien!*" And in fact,

IN THE CASINO, MONTE CARLO.

that night the man returned and lost, not only his eighty thousand dollars, but ten thousand more which he had borrowed.

These richly decorated halls are never empty during gaming hours. Around every table there is always a close circle of seated players, behind whom usually stand as many more, reaching over their shoulders to play.

Among those who lose the largest sums here are Russians, who have the reputation of playing recklessly. The French, principally Parisians, contribute largely to the crowd at the tables. Germans play considerably, but so cautiously that they are considered the least remunerative customers of the bank. Spaniards and Italians are comparatively few in number here; while, on the other hand, Americans outnumber the English, notwithstanding the proximity of Great Britain. Curiously enough, fully one half of the players are women of all ages and conditions of life. These do not seem to be able to preserve the equanimity usually characteristic of the gambler. Once, for example, when I had placed several small sums unsuccessfully on the color which an old lady beside me had also chosen, she turned to me very impatiently, and said that I was spoiling her luck.

It is a significant fact that the only people in the world who are deprived of the pleasure, or misery, of playing at roulette are the inhabitants of Monaco; for the Prince forbids his own subjects to enter the gambling-halls.

The most unpleasant feature of Monte Carlo,—the serpent in the paradise,—is the fact that tragedies frequently occur within its limits. It is said that a conservative estimate of the suicides that take place here would be six a month, and many maintain that twelve or fifteen would not be too high an average; for the employees maintain perfect silence regarding such "accidents," and the papers of Nice are bribed to say little or nothing of such matters. Moreover, the police have strict orders to search the grounds every morning for dead bodies, and to remove them as quickly as possible; and if a man loses all his money and seems desperate, the bank will gladly give him funds enough to enable him to cross the frontier and depart for home.

Not long ago, however, this generosity of the "Administration" was misused in an unexpected manner. One evening, when the play was at its fiercest, a stranger was seen to rush out of the Casino, with despair and madness evident in his excited strides, wild eyes, and ruffled hair. Soon the familiar bang! bang! of a revolver rang through the air; and one of the attendants, running in the direction of the sound, found the unfortunate stranger stretched out motionless in a secluded corner of the garden, the smoking revolver in his hand. At once, with great presence of mind, and in obedience to the rules of the Administration, he stuffed the

NÎMES.

pockets of the fallen man with bank-notes enough to convince
the most prejudiced observer that the catastrophe could not
have been the result of ruin at the tables, and then sped off
to give the alarm.   A few minutes later, a cloud of would-be
witnesses were on the spot, but, lo! there was nothing for
them to witness.   The stranger and the notes had vanished.

THE PUBLIC GARDEN, NÎMES.

The pretty manufacturing city of sixty thousand inhabitants in the south of France, which bears the name of Nîmes,
(or Nismes), retains in its contracted form, a reminder of its
Roman ancestor, "Nemausus."

"Nemausus!" the reader perhaps exclaims, "I never heard
of such a place."   Nor is it strange, for it was seldom mentioned by classical authors, and its origin is wrapped in obscurity; yet while many more celebrated cities have fallen into
complete ruin, Nemausus, or Nîmes, as it is now called, still
retains relics of its ancient splendor.

The most remarkable of these is its grand amphitheatre,
which is better preserved than the Colosseum at Rome.   Yet

what a series of misfortunes have its walls survived! Long
after the death of the Roman emperor during whose reign it
was founded, the Goths converted it into a fortress. The
Saracens also, at the beginning of the eighth century, en-
trenched themselves within its walls, until expelled by Charles
Martel, who himself endeavored to destroy the building by filling its many passages with wood, and setting it on fire. Then,
for centuries, a multitude of common people made their homes
within its corridors, until in 1810, when by order of Napoleon
the place was cleared, there had been constructed here no
less than three hundred houses, inhabited by some two thousand people.

I felt a deeper admiration for the architecture of the Romans, as I walked in these gigantic passageways, which
formerly swarmed with thousands of excited citizens going
to and from their seats. So vast are the proportions of this
amphitheatre, and so massively is it constructed, that it will
probably continue to exist for as many centuries as have
elapsed since its completion. Thus in these corridors are
hundreds of stone blocks eighteen feet long, yet fastened by
no cement. One feels that this was the work of men who
built with blocks of stone commensurate in size with their
gigantic plans. What perfect means the Romans always
provided to facilitate the egress of their multitudes! Here,
for example, there were no less than sixty enormous arch-
ways opening from the outside corridor, and every passage
leading into this from the interior was of great breadth, and
widened outwards; so that the building, colossal though it
was, could in a few minutes be easily emptied of its twenty
thousand spectators. The structure is astonishingly well preserved, and hundreds of the old seats, are almost as perfect
as when their occupants, in bloodthirsty excitement, gazed
downward from them into the arena, now so silent and deserted.

On the topmost circle we saw the places for the gilded posts from which an enormous awning was stretched above the assembled multitude. We also peered shudderingly into the dark dens where formerly wild beasts were made still wilder, and where gladiators, or possibly martyrs, awaited the signal which should summon them to struggle for their lives.

Not far from the amphitheatre stands a very different relic of the Roman citizens of Nîmes. It is now known merely as the *Maison Carrée*, but this name gives one no idea of its former use. It was originally a small but elegant Corinthian temple, dating

CORRIDOR IN THE AMPHITHEATRE.

probably from the reign of Antoninus Pius, but possibly from the era of Augustus. It is evident, too, that it was connected with other buildings whose foundations are still plainly visible, and probably formed part of the Forum of the city. A veritable gem of architecture this must once have been; for, notwithstanding its mutilation, one can plainly discern upon its walls the outlines of a delicately sculptured frieze, and its thirty elegant Corinthian columns show many traces of their former beauty. It has known strange vicissitudes in its eventful history; for it has served in turn as a pagan temple, a Christian church, a convent, a tomb, a Revolutionary tribunal, a warehouse, and even as a stable. But it has been finally rescued from neglect and vandalism and transformed into a museum of antiquities.

Upon a hill above the city we saw another strange memento of the Past in a mysterious monument, nearly one hundred feet in height, the origin of which is still a matter of dispute. It once undoubtedly formed part of the ancient wall of the city, built by Augustus nineteen hundred years ago; but whether it was merely a tower of defense, or possibly a princely mausoleum, is unknown.

An interior staircase leads to the summit, and climbing thither we enjoyed a charming view of the Public Gardens of Nîmes, thickly planted with shade-trees, among which are several handsome fountains. Standing upon this ruin, nearly twenty centuries old, and looking down upon the city, I realized what a singular blending there is here of the ancient and the modern. For closely adjoining the beautiful gardens, handsome boulevards, and bright cafés which make of Nîmes a miniature Paris, are monuments which forcibly

THE ANCIENT TOWER. NÎMES.

remind one that pagan Rome still lives here, though apparently dead, and that at every step we tread the dust of the old Roman World.

Thus in one corner of the park, where children romp and Offenbach's music floats upon the air, are the remains of a

graceful Roman temple, dedicated to the nymphs, and built here during the reign of Augustus; and one can see within its walls, upon a marble altar, some of the old bronze vessels, half corroded from age and exposure, on which the priests formerly burned incense to the fair deities of the waters. The principal fountain also of the park

THE RUINED TEMPLE OF THE NYMPHS.

on which the modern tourist looks with pleasure, supplied a Roman bath at Nîmes, and at the time of Christ, poured forth its limpid stream as freely as it does to-day.

Even if Nîmes itself were uninteresting, which it is far from being, it would well repay the traveler to halt here, if only to visit, a few miles distant, one of the finest relics of her power which ancient Rome has left in Europe,—the Pont du Gard. I shall never forget the moment when, turning the corner of a sombre gorge, I suddenly beheld above a

mass of oaks and olive-trees the form of this stupendous Roman aqueduct. It is a granite chain uniting two mountains, and crossing the gleaming waters of the river Gard in a series of perfectly preserved arches, the highest of which rises one hundred and sixty feet above the gorge. Of all the Roman aqueducts that I have ever seen, including that of Segovia in Spain, none has impressed me like the Pont du Gard. So solidly is it constructed, that even now,

THE FOUNTAIN AT NÎMES.

after the lapse of nineteen hundred years, it is still well-nigh perfect, and joins the opposite hills with skillfully fitted blocks of stone, so huge that one conjectures in amazement how they could ever have been placed in their position.

Eighteen years before the Christian era, Marcus Agrippa, the son-in-law of the Emperor Augustus, ordered his soldiers to supply the city of Nîmes with water from two copious springs twenty-five miles away. The Pont du Gard itself is, therefore, only a fragment of the whole canal of solid masonry

THE PON. DU GARD

through which the water came; for the entire conduit was twenty-five miles long, and after spanning valleys, tunneling rocks, surmounting hills, and even passing for long distances underground, poured forth at last the water which it had conveyed, now through the earth, and now among the clouds.

We climbed the hill, and stood upon the highest bar of this leviathan of masonry, and here, within the very channel where for sixteen hundred years the water flowed unchecked to Nîmes, we walked from cliff to cliff! For it is still a perfectly preserved canal, no less than seven feet in height and four in breadth, and lined on both sides with a calcareous deposit, six inches thick, left atom by

THE ROMAN AQUEDUCT.

atom by the water as it flowed along for hundreds of years after the Roman Empire itself had passed away. We lingered here until the sun went down in majesty behind the lonely hills. Before it disappeared, however, it seemed to pause and turn on this gigantic framework of the Past an ardent, lingering gaze, which flooded it with glory. I shall never forget how beautiful this multitude of noble arches looked, as the western sky grew golden, and these massive bars stood out in picturesque relief against the radiant light. Towering above the desolate river which was dark with shadows, the mighty structure seemed the *soul* of the whole

landscape; and as I gazed upon the highest arch, which had
for centuries held within its breast a crystal artery of life, pul-
sating ceaselessly beneath a subtle force born in the mountains
far away, time seemed for a moment to have been annihil-
ated, and once again in this small corner of the Roman empire, and after nearly two millenniums of history, the Pont
du Gard bore splendid testimony to the power of the Eternal
City, proclaiming it to be still, as in the days of Augustus,
Mistress of the World.

SPAIN

THE ALHAMBRA HILL.

Spain

A HALF century ago, a tour in Spain was regarded as a dangerous enterprise. Even the Spaniards themselves, when about to travel in their own country, first, by way of preparation, sent for a priest to absolve their sins, a doctor to give them medicine, and a lawyer to make their wills. In recent years, however, traveling conveniences there have been so improved that priest, physician, and advocate are now no longer deemed so indispensable for a Spanish journey as a full purse and a reliable guide-book. Nevertheless, although it is easy of access and scarcely to be surpassed in interest by any other country on the globe, comparatively few tourists visit Spain. These few, however, are abundantly repaid. A Spanish preacher

A SPANISH DILIGENCE.

once declared that when Satan conveyed the Son of Man to the top of an exceedingly high mountain and showed to Him the kingdoms of the world, it was fortunate that Spain was hidden from view behind the Pyrenees, for otherwise (in his opinion) the temptation would have been irresistible.

Does one desire sublime and varied scenery? In Spain it is spread broadcast, skirted by the classic Mediterranean and canopied by a sky of incomparable depth and beauty. Beneath its azure dome not only bloom the olive, the pomegranate, the orange, and the palm; but there, in striking contrast, are rugged mountains, and savage, solitary plains, imposing and majestic even in their severity. Is one in quest of art? Many of the grandest cathedrals in the world rear in Spain their vast proportions; while her famous picture-gal-

THE BRIDGE BETWEEN FRANCE AND SPAIN.

lery at Madrid is equal to any in Italy, and superior to all the rest in Europe. Does one seek historic interest? Then surely Spain will prove no disappointment, for ruined structures, dating back to Romans, Goths, and Moors, are still extant there, fanned by the perfumed breath of orange-trees, or shaded by the drooping fringes of the palm, and speaking to us of the successive dominion of many powerful races, each of which has left behind it indestructible evidences of its sway. From Spain have come forth men destined to wield, as Roman emperors, the sceptre of the world. Here, too, the gifted Moors maintained their brilliant court for seven hundred years; and after their expulsion, there were times when Europe trembled at the nod of Spain and when her commerce was supreme. In fact, powerful in Germany, mistress of Italy, Belgium, and Holland, victorious over France, and drawing countless treasures from her colonies, Spain seemed at one time the dominant nation on the globe; while the discovery of America by Columbus and of India by Da Gama, together with her conquests in the New World under Cortez and Pizarro, not only shone like stars on the escutcheon of her history, but placed for years in her controlling hands the destinies of the two hemispheres.

It will always be to me a memorable day when, from the southern province of the French republic, I crossed for the first time that majestic boundary between France and Spain—the Pyrenees. Never have I beheld from a railroad train such glorious mountain vistas as those which greeted us at every turn while winding up the Pyrenean heights. The ascent is gradual, but constant; for the centre of Spain is an immense plateau, rising in several places more than two thousand feet above the level of the sea. From whatever direction, therefore, the traveler approaches Madrid, he must ascend to this lofty elevation. Over these mountain ranges,

TRAVELING THROUGH THE PYRENEES.

the Spanish railroads, which are splendid specimens of engineering skill, have been constructed at enormous expense and with the greatest difficulty. When once the mountain scenery is passed, however, the railway journey becomes monotonous. Spanish trains run slowly, make frequent stops, and

have a fashion of leaving prominent places at such unseasonable hours as three, four, or five o'clock in the morning, which after a time would certainly prove ruinous even to the sweetest of American dispositions. We observed beggars at every station and peasants in all degrees of rags and poverty.

A TOWER OF THE BURGOS CATHEDRAL.

The principal business at these halting places seemed to be that of selling cooling drinks to the passengers. The hot-blooded Spaniards seem always thirsty, and absorb liquids like sponges. Possibly this may be a consequence of their continuous smoking; for, mingled with the cries of *Agua, agua fresca!* [Water, fresh water!] are those of *Fósforos, fósforos!* [Matches, matches!] and both fire and water seemed equally in demand. I

wonder if a Spaniard exists who does not use tobacco! Some
wit has said that to a Spaniard a cigar is a cloud by day and
a pillar of fire by night; and that the tobacco-plant springs
spontaneously from every Spaniard's grave.

The beautiful cathedral at Burgos tempted us to break
the journey midway between the frontier and Madrid, and
spend twenty-four hours in the capital of Old Castile.   I
have never been quite certain whether to be glad or sorry
that we did so.   For pleasant and unpleasant memories are
suggested by the thought of Burgos.   It was the witching
hour of half-past three in the morning when we arrived there,
and the same hour the next morning when we resumed our
journey, since there was but one express train daily.   It was
dark and cold when we dragged our cramped limbs to the
hotel omnibus and yawned and shivered while the porter
piled our baggage on the roof.   Then, with much plunging
and floundering, some half-starved mules pulled the lumber-
ing vehicle over a series of rough pavements, and finally
brought up in front of the hotel with a jerk that almost threw
the passengers in a heap upon the floor.   We had come to the

THE MONUMENT TO THE CID, BURGOS.

only hotel in Burgos that the guide-books had dared to mention, and started bravely through an open door; but we soon discovered that we had entered a stable by mistake. Accordingly, trying a less inviting portal, we stumbled up some straw-covered stairs to a desolate upper hall. A sputtering oil-lamp winked an inflamed eye at us from the wall, but not a human being was visible. We therefore lifted up our

A BEAUTIFULLY SCULPTURED PORTAL.

voices, "*Fondista! Fondista!*" [Landlord! Landlord!] rang through the dismal halls, but all was silent as the grave. In despair we appealed to our omnibus driver, who, finally, with an air of conferring a great favor, condescended to show us some apartments. For a time we walked in desperation after this Spanish youth, from one room to another, each of which was a pungent reminder of the stable beneath. As each door was opened, it was as if a new bottle of unsavory odors had been uncorked, and when we stepped within, it seemed as if the bottle were held to our noses. At last, when we had chosen the least offensive rooms, daylight was streaming through the broken shutters, and wrapping the draperies of our couches about us, we lay down to unpleasant dreams.

The great object of attraction in Burgos which induces tourists to put up with such discomforts is its cathedral of

IN THE BURGOS CATHEDRAL.

white marble — unquestionably one of the noblest specimens
of Gothic architecture in the world.   Its pointed towers rise
like slender pyramids into the blue air to the height of three
hundred feet, and are so exquisitely cut in perforated stone,
that by night the stars gleam through the chiseled tracery as
through the trees.   Its splendid central tower resembles a
grand tiara, adorned with scores of pinnacles and statues and
turrets of wonderful lightness.   This elaborate carving and
wealth of decoration reminded us of the Milan cathedral, and
we could hardly wonder at Philip II's declaration, that parts
of it seemed the work of angels rather than of men.

An extraordinary object in this sanctuary is the old
treasure-chest, or strong-box, of the Cid.
Burgos is proud of having been the birth-
place of this hero, and guards his coffer
as a priceless relic.   Although the Cid
has been for nearly nine hundred years
the national hero of the Spaniards, and
a kind of modern Hercules, there is no
doubt that he was a real
character, whose exploits
have been embellished and
exaggerated by a mass of
fables till, in the legends of
old Spain, his name, like
that of Abou ben Adhem,
" led all the rest."   He
seems to have been a kind
of free-lance, — a demigod
for subsequent banditti, —
warring alike on Moor and
Christian to advance his own
interests, and always equally feared by both.   Certainly

STATUE OF PHILIP IV, MADRID.

the " Poem of the Cid," composed in the twelfth century, is
the oldest book of Spanish poetry extant, and it is said that
a larger number of ballads have been devoted to his history
than to any other subject.

Somebody has said that the king who first made Madrid
a court residence, cannot yet have gotten out of purgatory,
so great was the evil inflicted thereby on the nation.　As a

matter of fact,
three centuries
ago Madrid was
an insignificant
hamlet. Toledo
and Seville had
been in turn
the capitals of
Spain : one seat-
ed like a king
upon a rocky

THE BRIDGE AT MADRID.

throne ; the
other rising queen-like from the Guadalquivir, to send her
fleets along its silver tide, far out upon the broad Atlantic.
But, unfortunately, those were days when one man's whims
might affect a nation's welfare; and since Charles V had
fewer twinges of the gout in the sharp air of this locality, he
chose it as the home of royalty, though Roman, Goth, and
Moor had all alike rejected it.　Notwithstanding its enormous
bridge, it is a farce to claim that Madrid is situated on a
river; for the Manzanares, which looked to us like the sea-
shore when the tide is out, is really nothing but a mountain
stream, so dry for three-fourths of the year that the washer-
women can hardly procure enough water from it to cleanse the
linen of Madrid.　It is highly amusing, therefore, to see ponderous arches spanning the little brook; but they are said to

be needful when the mountain snows are melting, since then
the swollen stream, for a time, threatens to carry everything
before it. When Napoleon's soldiers, in pursuit of the fugitive Spaniards, came to the Manzanares, they exclaimed:
"What! Do Spanish rivers run away, too?" The Spaniards
themselves joke about this feature of Madrid. One, for example, compares this river's god, whose urn is so often dry,
to the rich man in hell calling in vain for one drop of water;
and it is a standing joke that the king ought either to buy
another river or else sell his bridge.

The climate of Madrid is far from healthful. It has been
called "nine months hibernal and three months infernal."
Built on the highest point of the great table-land, which forms
the centre of the peninsula, it lies two thousand four
hundred feet above the sea. There are no forests near, to
break the force of the piercing winds from the neighboring
snow-capped mountains; and though in summer the sun is

THE "GATEWAY OF THE SUN," MADRID.

often as scorching as a blast from a fiery furnace, by crossing
to the shady side of the street one may feel cool enough for
an overcoat or shawl. The difference between sun and shade
is sometimes twenty degrees. After a little experience,

therefore, we began to appreciate the Spanish proverb—"The air of Madrid will not blow out a candle, but it kills a man."

Soon after our arrival in the Spanish capital, we found ourselves in the famous square of Madrid,—the Puerta del Sol. This "Gateway of the Sun" was formerly the eastern portal of the city, and hence the first to be greeted by the dawn, but now it marks the centre of the great metropolis. As our hotel was situated here and we could view it at any hour of the day or night, we soon discovered the cause of its

THE ROYAL PALACE, MADRID.

celebrity. For, although neither beautiful nor imposing, it constitutes the very heart of Madrid and throbs with tireless activity. Here are the best cafés, and the most important banking-houses, in front of which the devotees of pleasure or of business pass to and fro incessantly. Donkeys with tinkling bells, bull-fighters with sombreros, beggars with outstretched hands, and Castilians with folded cloaks, were visible here from dawn to dusk. From time to time wild-looking peasants would appear, making the hot air vibrate with their cries, as they proclaimed their wares for sale. Accompanying them were usually half a dozen mules, which, with their closely shaven backs, looked like gigantic rats. Around the walls a score of men and boys were constantly acquiring fresh coats of tan by sleeping in the sun; and as for priests, the square seemed fairly alive with their three-cornered hats and long black robes, which make them look like monster crows.

If you are in a mood for it, the sight of this animated, sunlit plaza makes you gay; if not, and, above all, if you are here alone, it renders you more sad than would the desert; for you well know that in this motley throng that crowds the Gateway of the Sun, there is not one who knows your name, or cares about your existence or your death.

STAIRCASE IN THE ROYAL PALACE, MADRID.

The Royal Palace in Madrid is universally conceded to be one of the most imposing kingly residences in the world. I can recall but two which are comparable to it: the Winter Palace of the Tsar at St. Petersburg, and one of the Sultan's marble structures on the Bosporus. Its splendid staircase of black and white marble is one of the finest in Europe, and so broad on either side that twenty men abreast could easily ascend it. When Napoleon entered this palace as conqueror of Spain, he is said to have placed his hand on one of these balustrades, exclaiming eagerly, "At last I have this Spain so long desired." Then, gazing on the magnificence before him, he turned to his brother Joseph, whom he had just made King of Spain, remarking: "My brother, you will be better lodged than I."

The throne-room is of enormous size and lavishly adorned. The floor is of marble mosaic, and from the ceiling, which

THE THRONE-ROOM.

is richly painted and gilded, are suspended huge chandeliers of rock-crystal. The walls, too, are lined with mirrors set in costly marbles; and at every turn one looks on exquisite vases, bronzes, and statuary.

There are, however, few historical associations to lend value to this splendor. The frivolous, dissipated lives which have been led here are hardly worth the trouble of investigation; and, in her sad decadence, Spain has seen little issue from this room save a succession of inglorious reigns. Poor Spain! She has been long and systematically misruled. Bad Governments have well-nigh ruined her.

There is a tradition that King Ferdinand, on being presented to the Holy Virgin after death, asked for his country a long succession of favors, all of which were granted. At last, however, having begged for a good Government, the

THE ROYAL ARMORY.

Virgin refused him pointblank. "If I gave you that," she replied, "not an angel would remain with me in Paradise; they would migrate at once to Spain!"

One remarkable feature of this palace is the surprising number of clocks that it contains. There are, if I remember rightly, no less than five in one anteroom alone. In many apartments there are twice as many. A wit has said that this is the more extraordinary, as Spanish sovereigns have always been proverbially behind time. However this may be, some of them have had a mania for collecting clocks. Charles V, especially, bought scores of them, in his determination to make two go precisely alike; but, failing in this after

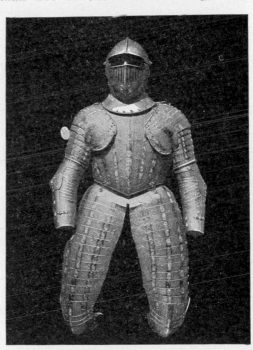

THE ARMOR OF CHRISTOPHER COLUMBUS.

repeated trials, he confessed that it was equally impossible to make men's minds hold exactly the same opinions.

Another very interesting portion of this palace is its celebrated armory. On crossing its threshold we were confronted by an army of warlike effigies — on horseback, and on foot — including kings, emperors, and famous heroes, clad in the finest suits of armor ever made. The walls, too, were covered with helmets, battle-axes, lances, swords, antique muskets, and coats of mail; while from the ceiling hung a multitude of tattered flags, trophies of victories gained in many portions of the globe. Some of these relics have a personal interest connected with the men who wore or wielded

STATUE OF CERVANTES, MADRID.

them. Thus we beheld here the swords of Cortez and Pizarro, the conquerors of Mexico and Peru. Here are magnificent Toledo blades which belonged to Charles V and Philip II. Beside them hangs a suit of armor worn by poor Boabdil, the last of the Moorish sovereigns of Granada. Here also can be seen the armor of Columbus; the sword which King Ferdinand carried in his battles with the Moors; and the litter on which Charles V was carried about when old and suffering. Truly, a soul-stirring room is this old Spanish armory. As I walked through its corridors glistening with steel, I felt myself carried back to the heroic days of Spain,—the age of her conquests and her glory. For here are the swords of her ablest leaders, the helmets of her most intrepid discoverers, and the breastplates beneath which her most valiant hearts have throbbed.

Another prominent building in Madrid is the House of Parliament. Before this, in the centre of the square, stands a bronze statue of Spain's greatest literary genius,—the author of the immortal Don Quixote — Cervantes. I was surprised to see him represented with a military cloak and sword; but a little reflection convinced me that these are not unsuited to that man of letters, for in his youth Cervantes

was a gallant soldier, and bore the scars of battle till his
death.   And yet this man who had shed his blood freely for
his country, and who has caused the world to call the Spanish tongue "the language of Cervantes," was miserably poor
in life, and was buried like a pauper.   By a strange coincidence, he died on the very day when the soul of the great
Shakespeare also passed away from earth.   How little did
the world then realize its great loss!   For more than a hundred years after Cervantes' death the places of his birth and
burial were unknown; and only centuries after the hand that
wrote and the brain that labored were but dust, was he hon-
ored throughout the world in song and story and by his
statue in the Spanish capital.

The great rendezvous of fashionable life in Madrid corresponding to the Champs-Élysées of Paris, is the Prado,—a
promenade two and a half miles long, which, as the name in-
dicates, was once
an extensive
meadow.   On
summer even-
ings, this be-
comes a kind of
open-air draw-
ing-room, fre-
quented by the
best society of
the capital.   It
is a charming
place for ro-
mance; for in
the favoring

IN THE PRADO, MADRID.

twilight the ladies are all beautiful and every cavalier is handsome.   The heat and turmoil of the day are gone, and, since
the Madrid world has already enjoyed an afternoon siesta,

no one desires to retire early, and music floats upon the air from half past nine till after midnight. Here one sees many friendly groups or family parties gathered by themselves, and, in the pauses of the orchestra, the hum of conversation is borne upon the breeze, mingled with the sharp rustle of the ladies' fans, which open and close incessantly, as skillful fingers move them with wonderful rapidity and grace. Apparently the young men of Madrid bestow much time and care upon their toilettes, for they look as if they had just stepped out of a tailor's establishment and were wearing their fine clothes for the first time. It was only in the mature Spaniards, as a rule, that I saw indications of strong character or serious thought. The sight of some of these Spanish exquisites idling along the Prado recalled the remark of a dignified, turbaned Moor to his son, when he first saw a perfumed, effeminate dandy: "My son," he solemnly exclaimed, "if you ever forget your God and Prophet, and forsake the religion of your fathers, may you come to look like that!"

Even the children in the Prado were richly dressed. Soon after our arrival in Madrid a festival was held for the little ones in Spain. The streets were full of lovely children, dressed with elegance and decorated with brilliant colors. Several of them ran up to me on the Prado and held out tiny plates in their little gloved hands. At first I could not understand this, although I willingly gave the coin which they asked for. But I was afterward informed that on this particular day Spanish children are allowed thus to solicit small coins from adults to buy for themselves bonbons, dolls, and toys.

The most prominent building in the Prado is its picture-gallery. Before I went to Spain, a gentleman assured me that I would find the picture-gallery in Madrid superior to any in the world. "Not better than any in Italy!" I exclaimed incredulously. "Yes," he replied, unhesitatingly,

"superior to any in the world." I came to Madrid still
skeptical on this point, but having seen the gallery I am entirely of his opinion. Just at the time when art was flourishing in the Netherlands, Spain was the sovereign power in
those countries. Hence many of the finest works of Dutch
and Flemish artists found their way to the court of Philip II.
Whatever may be said in criticism of Spanish monarchs, it

THE PICTURE-GALLERY, MADRID.

must be admitted that they were fond of art and rich enough
to buy anything they wished for. Thus in the period of her
glory, Spain purchased an enormous number of fine paintings,
which subsequently were so effectually hidden away in palaces
and convents that men knew nothing of them; but now that
they have been brought together in Madrid they form a
collection of masterpieces unequaled in the world. Upon
the walls of this museum are hung no less than forty-six
paintings by Murillo, ten by Raphael, sixteen by Guido,
forty-three by Titian, sixty-four by Velasquez (whom Philip

IV called "my only painter"), twenty-five by Veronese, thirty-four by Tintoretto, sixty-two by Rubens, and fifty-three by Teniers, not to mention numberless other treasures. Truly, the day when a lover of art enters such a gallery as this marks an epoch in his life. The visions of beauty which

THE ESCORIAL.

surround him here will leave their influence upon him as long as memory lasts. Some one has said that, if a man knew that he would become blind in a year, there is no place where he could garner up so precious a store of memories for the days of darkness as in the Museum of the Prado.

Chief among the artists represented here is, of course, Murillo, of whom the Spaniards say that he painted flesh tints with milk and blood. Murillo is not really known outside of Spain. I had always supposed, for example, that his famous "Immaculate Conception" in the Louvre, which represents the Madonna standing on a silver crescent surrounded by a glittering garland of cherubs, whose faces fade away into a golden atmosphere of glory, was the noblest expression of Murillo's genius. Here, however, one gazes upon other "conceptions" by Murillo, even more lovely and tender than that. Moreover, what increases our enjoyment of these paintings is our comparative want of familiarity with them. With other works by Raphael, Titian, Murillo, and Guido one is already well acquainted, through photographs and engravings, if not by actual inspection. But of many of these Spanish masterpieces no engravings have ever been made, nor are photographs of them usually sold outside of Spain. Hence almost every picture is an unexpected revelation of beauty, and has the charm of a complete surprise. Anticipate what you will, you cannot be disappointed here. To have seen and studied them is a joy forever.

One of the most impressive days I passed in Spain was devoted to a visit to the Escorial, twenty-five miles distant from Madrid. To understand the origin and architecture of this combination of mausoleum and palace, one must take into consideration the fact that there once lived in this evil world a holy man known as St. Lawrence. He was, however, as unfortunate as he was holy, and wicked men put him on a gridiron and roasted him to death. Yet so undaunted was his courage, that after one side of his body had been thoroughly roasted, he is said to have calmly asked his torturers to turn him over and roast the other side. One day, about three hundred years ago, the Spanish sovereign, Philip II, gained a decisive victory over

MURILLO.

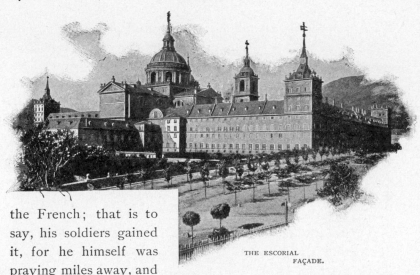

THE ESCORIAL
FAÇADE.

the French; that is to
say, his soldiers gained
it, for he himself was
praying miles away, and
ready to flee for his life in case of a defeat.   When victory
was assured, Philip, unwilling to give the credit to his general,
ascribed it to the influence of St. Lawrence, upon whose
anniversary the battle had been fought.   To honor the saint,
therefore, as well as to commemorate the victory, he reared
this grim leviathan of architecture.   There never was, and I
hope never will be, a gloomier building.   Even its situation
is appalling.   Of all the dreary places I have ever seen, except the desert of Sahara and the wilderness of Judea, this
carries off the palm for desolation.   On one side, savage-look-
ing mountains tower threateningly above the place, without a
particle of vegetation on their sides from base to summit; and
on the other is a dreary waste of sand and rocks, resembling
the lava-beds of old volcanoes.   Yet such a site is admirably
suited to the Escorial.   Cold as the heart of its founder, this
granite mass would have been out of keeping with the flowers
and sunshine of a fertile valley.   In honor of the roasted
saint, Philip ordered this palace to be made in the form of a
gridiron, and, as his will was law, this enormous structure, one
of the largest in the world, and called by the Spaniards the

eighth wonder of the world, was actually built after that grotesque design. Vast galleries, seven hundred feet in length,
cross it to represent the gridiron bars; an immense projection
on one side, containing the royal apartments, typifies the
handle; while the feet of the inverted gridiron are indicated
by pointed towers rising from the corners. The Escorial
is therefore a despot's frightful fancy petrified,—something
designed, apparently, by the author of the Inquisition during
his hours of sleeplessness or remorse.

We entered the Escorial by means of a door in one of the
gridiron bars. Over the study of the Grecian sage was written: "Let no one enter here who does not know geometry."
If I could inscribe a warning over the portal of the Escorial it
would be this: "Let no one enter here without a flask of
brandy." Do not smile and deem this idle counsel. I
had anticipated a cold place, and had put on an overcoat

A CORRIDOR IN THE ESCORIAL.

and gloves, so as to be prepared. But scarcely had we
crossed the threshold when we seemed to be pierced to the
very marrow with a death-like chill. There was no heat in
the entire building, which displayed at every turn nothing

but stone walls, stone ceilings, stone floors, and iron doors. It is impossible to describe the Escorial in detail, for this monstrous refrigerator has no less than sixteen granite court-yards, eighty granite staircases, twelve hundred doors, eleven thousand windows (to commemorate the eleven thousand

A COURT IN THE ESCORIAL.

virgins whose bones lie at Cologne), and, in all, about fifty miles of surface to walk over. I did not count all these, but I do not doubt the figures, and I am more certain of the fifty miles of walking than of anything else. Moreover, the Escorial is so terribly monot-onous in its eternal garb of granite, that I could with diffi-culty distinguish the halls I had seen from those which I had not. Even the eleven thousand windows are barricaded with iron gratings, and one hears nothing in the corridors but the hollow echo of his steps, like the laughter of ghosts. Nor is there any beauty to relieve the eye. It is true, there are a few frescoes representing the tortures of heretics in the flames of hell, but these are not at all beautiful, though

I am bound to say, they were the warmest things I found in
the Escorial.

There is, however, one minute part of this building which
looks habitable; for within the handle of the gridiron are a
few apartments, made cheerful after Philip II's time, so that
people could occasionally sleep here without danger of insan-
ity. Yet this cheerfulness is only superficial. Behind the
tapestries is the same cold granite, and just below these

PHILIP II'S CHAIRS.

rooms is the Pantheon, the burial-place of Spanish kings.
Into that crypt the light of day never penetrates; but, by the
glimmer of lamplight, we could see that the walls surrounding the gilded coffins of the Spanish sovereigns were lined
with porphyry, jasper, and agate. But oh! what words can
picture its unearthly chill? Compared with that, the temperature of the corridors seemed tropical. While standing there
with uncovered heads, it seemed to me that the skeleton of
Death was using my spine for a flute, running his icy fingers
up and down the vertebræ, and touching me here and there

with clammy hands. Our teeth chattered like the instruments in a telegraph office, and I asked no questions for fear of biting my tongue off. We were glad enough when the door of the Pantheon closed behind us, and we had left the gorgeous hall of Death in its mantle of everlasting darkness, and felt no more its piercing, glacial breath. It is, no doubt, a splendid sepulchre; but oh, rather than all that icy grandeur, give me a grave, however humble, beneath the open sky, where the air is perfumed by the breath of flowers and is musical with the song of birds!

The most interesting part of the Escorial is the portion which constituted the residence of Philip II. Particularly impressive was the bare, comfortless room where he died in agony, after he had been carried once more through these tomb-like halls, that he might bid farewell to the work of his life. On one side is the little window to which, on the morning of September 13, 1598, he dragged his emaciated form that he might fix his closing eyes upon the altar where mass was being said in the adjoining chapel. Here, grasping the same crucifix that Charles V had held in his last moments, this cruel and misguided bigot breathed his last, and, after forty years of tyranny and persecution, bequeathed to Spain a decay which has never since been checked.

In this room we saw the wooden chair on which he sat and boasted that from this wild mountain solitude he ruled two worlds. Beside it is the bench on which he placed his gouty limb, and on its leathern cover we discerned the imprint of that heel which during two-score years rested so heavily on half the world. After innumerable burnings and beheadings, Philip could boast here that not a heretic lived within his kingdom; but for the same reason that another tyrant was able to say to his confessor, who urged him on his death-bed to forgive his enemies: "Father, I have no enemies: I have killed them all."

The portrait of Philip II painted by Titian hangs in the Escorial. It is indeed the face of a man who is said to have laughed outright but once in his life, and that was when he heard of the massacre of St. Bartholomew. His cold, gray eyes have a hideous glitter of cruelty in them, and seem to possess no more warmth than the granite of the Escorial. At the same time, the picture is so lifelike that the grave seems to have given up its dead, and I felt, in looking at it, that I had at last come face to face with the pallid phantom which had apparently been following us everywhere with the stealthy footfall of a ghost. In imagination one can see him seated among the dreary boulders of the hillside, watching with eager eyes the progress of this edifice, as bar after bar was added to the granite gridiron. One recol-

PHILIP II.

lects, too, the remarkable scene when a messenger brought him the tidings of the destruction of the Spanish Armada, that fleet of invasion on which he had expended a hundred million ducats, and eighteen years of his life. The iron countenance of Philip remained unmoved, and looking up from his writing he answered merely:

"I thank God for having given me the means to bear this loss without embarrassment, and power to fit out another fleet of equal size. A stream can afford to waste some water when its source is not dried up."

I never shall forget how delightful it was to leave the

Escorial. When once again we breathed fresh air and saw the open sky, we laughed for joy. They seemed to be features of another world from which we had been exiled.

As we rode away from the prodigious edifice, our guide pointed out to us one of its corners into which Philip caused to be inserted a plate of gold an inch thick and a yard square. It was done in mere bravado. The Escorial had

CHURCH OF ST. JOHN OF THE KINGS, TOLEDO.

already cost the enormous sum of fifty million dollars, and the world predicted Philip's ruin. He, therefore, needlessly inserted here the precious metal to show his critics that he had gold enough to waste. Fortunately for its preservation it is above the dome, and glitters inaccessible to thieves.

Théophile Gautier advises every one who thinks himself unhappy to go to the Escorial; for learning there how utterly wretched existence might be, he will be more contented all the rest of his life, from being able to say in the most deplorable circumstances: "I might be in the Escorial — and I am not."

Another very interesting excursion from Madrid was that which took us to the neighboring city of Toledo. Viewed from near or far, the situation of Toledo is magnificent. With the exception of Jerusalem, it is probably the most picturesquely located city in the world. Enthroned upon a rocky bluff twenty-four hundred feet above the sea, it rises almost perpendicularly from the river Tagus,

TOLEDO AND THE ALCÁZAR.

which, surging through a chasm in the granite hills, girdles the city almost completely.

The hill on which Toledo stands is terraced with houses, churches, palaces, convents, and old Moorish walls and towers, till finally the summit is surmounted by the enormous, orange-colored citadel of the Alcázar, frowning for miles over the surrounding plain.

What wonder that with such a situation Toledo has been besieged more than a score of times? What marvel that

every conqueror who beholds it covets and resolves to have
it? This gloomy castle-crowned city possesses an eventful
history. Founded long before the Christian era by the Phœni-
cians, it was afterward a place of refuge for the Jews, who fled
hither after the
destruction of
Jerusalem, only
to find this city
also ruled by the
all-conquering
Romans. Then
came the Goths,
who drove the
Romans out of
Spain, as they
had previously
crushed Rome
in Italy. These
were succeeded

OLD BRIDGE AT TOLEDO.

by the Moors, who, perched like eagles on these rocky heights,
bade defiance to their foes for centuries. But finally they
too were driven forth by another set of conquerors,—the
Christians, who, having gained possession of these historic
cliffs, have ever since retained them.

Around this Spanish town are several picturesque bridges,
which, one after the other, in the course of centuries, have
flung across the Tagus their gigantic forms. With one of
these, erected more than seven hundred years ago to replace
a Moorish structure, is connected a singular story of womanly
stratagem. It seems that the architect discovered, when too
late, that his work was not strong enough, and must inevitably fall under a heavy weight. To his wife alone he whispered his unhappy secret. "All is not lost," exclaimed the
lady of Toledo, "trust me, and you can still retrieve yourself."

Accordingly that very night she caused the bridge to
be set on fire, and by burning down the entire structure
saved her husband's reputation; for, profiting by his former
error, he made in the construction of this arch no such fault.

Less ancient than this, but wonderfully graceful, is the
bridge of Alcántara, which spans the Tagus in a single arch.
Near this point formerly lived that lovely girl whose charms
were destined to overthrow the Gothic empire in Spain.   The
last of the Gothic kings who sat upon the throne of Toledo
was Roderick, the base betrayer of an innocent maiden
entrusted to him by her father, who was his intimate friend.
The father of the injured girl implored the Moors to avenge
him, and, nothing loth, the Saracens advanced to attack
Toledo.   The Gothic sovereign went forth to meet them in
a chariot of ivory, and dressed in gold and purple, but soon,
in spite of his magnificence, suffered ignominious defeat

THE BRIDGE OF ALCÁNTARA.

and death on the banks of the Guadalquivir at the hands of
the resistless Moors.

Beyond the portcullis and tower which mark the two extremities of the bridge, the road winds gradually around the

hill like an Alpine pass, up to the Alcázar, a stronghold that has sheltered many conquerors. This was once so magnificent, alike in decoration and dimensions, that Charles V, when he first entered it, exclaimed: "To-day I feel as

IN THE ALCÁZAR OF TOLEDO.

never before that I am an Emperor and a King." But the ravages of time and man have so defaced its stately halls that the old fortress-palace is nothing but a shell of granite, looking profoundly desolate above the lonely river.

We entered Toledo by the Gateway of the Sun. It is a splendid relic of its ancient glory,—an eloquent reminder of the fact that formerly this city was the pride of Spain, as famous in the world as Constantinople or Damascus. It was the favorite city of the exiled Jew, the stronghold of the Goth, the metropolis of the Moor, and the capital of the Christian, and it still bears the seal of grandeur in its walls and towers. Yet when I passed beneath this Moorish arch, although it was the hour of noon, few people were visible; the grass was growing in the neighboring pavement, the sleep of a thousand years seemed to have fallen upon the inhabitants. *Ilium fuit!* The glory of Toledo has departed.

A TOLEDO STREET.

Once in our walks through this city of the past, we heard a rumbling like distant thunder, which gradually came nearer and nearer, startling us by its contrast to the usual tomb-like stillness of the place. The cause was soon apparent. It was the hotel omnibus—one of the few vehicles of which Toledo can boast. We were in one of the comparatively broad streets, yet had to step into a doorway to avoid being crushed by the passing wheels, which almost grazed the houses in their course.

On both sides of the Toledo streets rise tall houses, severe and melancholy in appearance, solid as citadels and pierced with occasional grated windows. The dwellings are not open here as in the south of Spain. No charming courtyards reveal their flowers and fountains behind trellises of open iron-work. On the contrary, the gateways look like the portals of a fortress, flanked as they are with granite columns, while their heavy oaken doors are studded with enormous nails. Usually two ponderous iron knockers hang upon these doors—one to be used by pedestrians, the other, much higher, for horsemen. Everything in Toledo seems sombre, stern, and mysterious. It is a city of the past,—almost as sad and silent as a tomb. I can recall no town more utterly devoid of modern characteristics. It is the ghost of a departed glory.

A TOLEDO DOORWAY.

Spain is richer in cathedrals than any other country in the world, and one of the grandest of them all is at Toledo. The Virgin Mary is said to have a special liking for it, and to have paid it frequent visits—on one occasion actually descending for the special purpose of putting a new robe on St. Ildefonso, one of the archbishops. In fact, the scene is represented in sculpture and painting in all parts of the cathedral, and, to preclude all doubt about it, the very stone is shown on which the Virgin alighted. It is encased in red marble, and over it is the inscription: "We will worship in the place where her feet have stood."

There are several statues of the Virgin in the Toledo

cathedral, each of which possesses a gorgeous toilette. One wears a mantle upon which are embroidered seventy-eight thousand pearls. Not content with that, the same statue is adorned with many diamonds, rubies, and emeralds. Her crown alone cost more than twenty-five thousand dollars, and her bracelets are valued at half that sum. All these are presents from kings and queens, popes, archbishops, and private ladies of wealth. Nor is this strange; for the Virgin ranks as a queen in Spain, and always wears the royal crown.

The grand proportions and beautiful architecture of the cathedral of Toledo cannot be too highly praised. After the bright glare of the Spanish sunlight, it was a pleasure to find ourselves in the grateful twilight of the interior, for its seven hundred and fifty iris-colored windows flood the vast edifice with a beautiful combination of light and shade. The pavement

A DOOR OF THE CATHEDRAL OF TOLEDO.

is of variegated marble, and around the walls are twenty-three elaborate chapels. The greatest artists of Spain labored on this cathedral for six centuries. It is not strange, therefore that it excited our enthusiasm. The choir, for example, is decorated with probably the most elaborate wood-carving in the world. Around a pavement of white marble rise, on

THE CARVED STALLS IN THE CATHEDRAL.

three sides, two rows of seats for the priests, one above the other. Their arms, back, feet, head-pieces, and railings are exquisitely carved into sacred, grotesque, mythological, or historical subjects in bas-relief. The upper row is the work of the cel-ebrated rivals, Berruguete and Philip of Borgona, who under-took their tasks, each determined to excel the other. One carved the seats on one side of the choir, the other the oppo-site ones. It is difficult to say which sculptor deserves the palm; but it is safe to say that no other wood-carving in Spain, rich as its cathedrals are in this respect, is equal to these sacerdotal chairs at Toledo. Moreover, to enhance their beauty, these seats are separated by beautiful jasper pillars, with alabaster bases and capitals; and over them extends a se-ries of medallions, with figures of saints and patriarchs in relief.

Leaving this splendid work of mediæval artists, we entered one of the side aisles of the cathedral. As these approach the head of the Latin cross which forms the ground-plan of the edifice, they wind about the high altar in a curve

which is not only charming from its grace, but awe-inspiring
from its lofty and majestic sweep. As we advanced along
this stately avenue, there burst upon our view a sight that
hushed our voices into whispers, and held us spellbound
where we stood. The lofty roof of the cathedral seemed to
have opened, and there, in the glory of ten thousand sun-
beams, we saw a multitude of angels, cherubs, saints, and
apostles, apparently descending from the opened skies. For
an instant the illusion was as perfect as if we were witnessing
a celestial vision. The cause was soon explained. Directly
behind the high altar is a circular opening in the ceiling,
through which the light freely enters. Around and within

this, as far as the
eye can reach,
have been sculp-
tured a multi-
tude of marble
figures, whose
appearance is
that of saints
and angels de-
scending on
the clouds of
heaven. In no
other cathedral
of the world
have I ever seen
such a design,
and I can recall
few more effect-
ive. Possibly

A SUPERB VISTA.

at some other time the impression might have been different.
But we beheld it when the long aisles were darkening in the
twilight and the storied windows glowed like tablets of rubies

and eralds. At such an hour, the statues in this lofty passage way through which the rays of sunset poured like a noiseless cataract of gold, appeared the wondrous revelation of another world.

I shall never forget the moment when we stood on one of the battlements of Toledo, and looked directly down upon the stern and melancholy Tagus, within whose depths were perfectly reflected the arches of a bridge gray with the mists of seven centuries. If there be a river in the world which has apparently failed to fulfil its mission, it is this. Designed by Nature to be the grand highway of Spain, it nevertheless flows on comparatively solitary and unused for many hundred miles. It might be made navigable to the sea, and thus connect interior Spain with Lisbon and the Atlantic. Yet for a great distance its waves are furrowed by no white-winged fleets; its waters reflect castles and dungeons instead of ports and warehouses, and scarcely a village rises from its banks. No commerce finds a channel here, and although its sands are reported to be in reality, as they are in appearance, golden, this misused river now flows idly on through barren plains, which the magic wand

CATHEDRAL OF TOLEDO.

of the Moor once made to blossom like a garden. Its sterile banks reminded us of the Spanish proverb: "The lark which would traverse this country must bring its own grain."

I can never forget the view which greeted us as we left Toledo on the edge of evening. Its mighty walls and tow- ers rose grandly above us, iso- lated from the rest of the world by the solitude of their sur- roundings, and

TOLEDO AND THE TAGUS.

standing out against the evening sky as solemn and mysterious as a vision of antiquity. Slowly the setting sun turned, one by one, the ripples of this river into a glittering pavement. Through the ruined towers of the Alcázar, it flung the ruddy glow of a conflagration, tinging them with that soft vermilion blush which only the southern sun can bestow upon the build- ings of the past. In that golden twilight the harsh outlines of its battlements grew soft and mellow, until the many scars inflicted there by time and man were all concealed; and glit- tering in the saffron west, the grand Alcázar looked like a vast sarcophagus of gold, in which the glory of dead empires lay entombed.

Bull-fighting must still be called the national amusement of the Spaniards, for bull-fights are even now patronized by royalty and nobility, and by thousands of men, women, and children in every large Spanish town. It was in Madrid that we saw our first bull-fight. In fact, on the very day of our arrival in the Spanish capital, we found the people in a perfect fever of excitement over the first combat of the season.

A SPANISH STREET SCENE.

In the hotels men talked of nothing else. Gigantic placards heralded the great event. Tickets were offered us at every turn, and even when we opened an American newspaper, the first words we beheld in it were these: "Wall Street excited! A strong bull market!"

Of course this bull-fight was to take place on Sunday. Most bull-fights do. The theology of the Spaniards is said to be something as follows: "As God worked six days and rested on the seventh, so we will rest six days and on the seventh go to the bull-fight." Scarcely has the sunburnt population risen from its knees at mass when it begins to clamor vociferously, "*Á los toros! Á los toros!*" [To the bulls! To the bulls!]

Our guide Patricio was strangely excited. "Come quickly, Señor," he exclaimed; "else I can get you no carriage. All the world goes to bull-fight to-day. Much crowd. Hurry, hurry, dear ladies!"

We scampered down the hotel steps, and seated ourselves in a carriage drawn by three gaily decorated mules harnessed abreast. Crack, crack, crack, went the coachman's whip, and away went our mules with their jingling bells, tearing madly through the streets, to the imminent danger of ourselves and everybody else; for all the mules and horses that day were going at full gallop. Soon we were out of the city gate and in the broad avenue leading to the amphitheatre.

BULL-FIGHTERS.

On that memorable Sunday afternoon it was swarming with people. The sidewalks, too, were crowded with excited, noisy pedestrians, eager to advance. They dared not, however, venture into the street, for that was full of vehicles. And such vehicles! All sorts of cabs, carts, omnibuses, and gaudily painted wagons, loaded down with people, were whirling along (sometimes six abreast), as if their drivers held a direct commission from the devil. One carriage in particular attracted great attention, for it contained four distinguished toreadors. Behind them on a horse, adorned with lavish decorations, came a showily dressed man, who was received with cheers.

"Who is he?" I inquired; "some prominent member of the Government?"

"He?" was the answer; "No, indeed! He is a more dis-

THE AMPHITHEATRE AT MADRID.

tinguished man to-day than any one of the queen's ministers:—he is the master of ceremonies for the bull-fight."

As we drew near the amphitheatre, our attention was called to two other heroes of the arena, surrounded by a gaping crowd. Their gorgeous dress would of itself have attracted the admiration of the populace; but in addition to this, these toreadors have often shown undoubted bravery when their lives hung on a single motion of the hand or foot. One of them was at that time the most distinguished matador in Spain; but no one would ever have supposed so from a view of his face. Fully aware that he was the observed of all observers, he wore a self-complacent smile of vanity. His plump cheeks betrayed no hint of training for athletic sports; but no doubt, like so many famous actors, if placed in the arena he would be in an instant quite transformed. The more I thought of this, the more I wished to see the transformation, and my desire was soon gratified. As we approached the entrance, Patricio pointed out to us some priests, who are always in attendance here to administer the sacrament to any dying bull-fighter. With this cheerful hint of what we were to see, we left our vehicle; which wheeled about while the last one of our party was still in the air, and rattled off in quest of other passengers. Then, guided by the skillful Patricio, we passed within the vast enclosure.

The bull-ring at Madrid is built after the style of an old Roman amphitheatre. It is nearly circular in form. Around the arena on the outside are corridors, with doors opening inwards toward the ring. Our seats were in the second story. We therefore ascended a flight of stairs and passed within the amphitheatre. A striking view outlined itself before us.

Around us on every hand was an unbroken, beautifully curving wall about a hundred feet in height. Below us was the arena; and between this and the top of the encircling wall was the most brilliant spectacle imaginable; for in the balconies and boxes were gathered no less than fifteen thousand people. Part of these were, of course, seated in the shade, and part in the sun, as the amphitheatre is entirely open to the sky. Some seats are exposed to the solar rays during the entire afternoon; but the Spaniards do not seem to mind it. At all events, on this occasion, six thousand Spanish sal-

SELECTING BULLS FOR THE ARENA.

amanders were assembled there, resigned to being grilled on their benches, if they could only see the noble sport. They naturally formed the most economical portion of the audience, for the sunny seats are cheapest, the shady ones the most expensive. Between the paradise of shade, however, and the inferno of the sun, is a small strip of purgatory, where, as the sun declines, some favored souls pass gradually from its torturing glare to cooler shadow. The price of purgatorial seats is therefore just midway between the others. As it was a question of money and not of merit, I found myself that day in paradise. The contrast between sunlight and shadow was most beautiful; for where the sunlight fell, six thousand brightly painted fans glittered with all the colors of the rainbow; while in the shade, the toilettes of the ladies, with their lovely black or white lace mantillas, were distinctly visible. It was one of those sights that for an instant make the heart beat almost to suffocation and cause one to catch his breath.

The murmur of thousands of voices, the cries of the venders of oranges and fresh water, and the cheers of eager spectators, as different movements were made preparatory to the combat, all formed a confused roar, comparable to nothing I had ever heard. At length, the shrill blast of a trumpet fell upon our ears. It was the signal for the arena to be cleared of all its lingering occupants. In a few moments the last man had left the enclosure. The arena was empty. Another flourish of trumpets, and in through one of the principal entrances marched the actors in the coming tragedy. At the head rode two picadors, lance in hand, and dressed in brilliant colors. Next came the chulos, bearing on their arms the scarlet cloaks with which it would be their duty to infuriate the bull. These were followed by four or five banderilleros, who were to act in a way which will be presently described. Last of all appeared, in the place of honor, the matadors, who give the bull his deathblow. The costumes of these men were peculiar. All except the picadors wore short breeches, silk stockings, and

vests and jackets embroidered with silver and gold.   Their
hair, which was very long, was arranged in a tight twist behind the head.   After the procession had crossed the arena,

it halted after the
manner of the
Roman gladia-
tors, before the
royal box and
made a saluta-
tion.   Then it
completed the

THE MATADOR'S CUNNING.

circuit of the
ring, the mata-
dors retiring from
the arena, while

A LEAP FOR LIFE.

the others took
various positions
about the bar-
rier.   Two offi-
cers, dressed in
black, and with
long nodding
plumes in their
hats, now rode

THE CHULO'S CLOAK.

in, and asked permission of the governor of the spectacle
to admit the bull.   The governor threw to them the key
of the den where the bull was confined, and riding rapidly

across the arena, the officers handed this to the keeper of the gate. While this was taking place I heard two persons directly behind me speaking English. "Harry," said a pleasant voice, "you know I have come here merely to please you. I think it is all horrid. I am not going to look at a thing in that arena. Moreover, remember, you promised to take me out if I feel faint."

"Faint!" was the reply; "nonsense! Just exercise your will-power, and you won't feel faint. If anything disagreeable happens, cover your face with your fan. Ah! there he comes!"

I heard a little scream, but had no time to look behind me; for the gate had suddenly swung open and a huge iron-gray bull had darted from a perfectly dark den into the arena. For a moment, dazzled by the sudden glare of light, astonished by the sight of the vast curving wall of human faces, and startled by the yells of thousands, he halted, his nostrils quivering. Then catching sight of the chulos, who at a safe distance were waving their red cloaks at him, he lowered his head and dashed furiously at them. Nimble as squirrels, these men leaped light-ly over the rail-ing of the arena into a circular

THE PICADOR'S ATTACK.

THE PICADOR'S OVERTHROW.

space beyond, and the bull stopped with a violent shock within
a foot of their retreating heels.   With a snort that denoted
mischief the bull glared around him.   Twenty feet away was
a picador on horseback.   Straight at him the bull now went.
The horse, whose eyes were blinded by a cloth, obedient to
his rider's spur, wheeled to one side, and the picador pressed
his lance into the bull's shoulder as he passed, inflicting only a
slight wound, however, for the iron on the lance is purposely
made very short.   The bull turned savagely about and, irritated
by the pain, charged once more upon the horse.   This time
the picador could do nothing, and both horns plunged deep
into the horse's side.   Ten thousand voices greeted this with
yells of approval.   "Bravo, Toro!   Bravo, Toro!" resounded
in deafening shouts from all parts of the arena.   This was
bad enough, but I felt almost faint when I saw the bull, by
a tremendous effort, lift both horse and rider from the
ground and roll them over in the dust.   All was at once a
frenzy of excitement.   The bull drew out his dripping horns
and prepared for a new charge.   If he made it, it would be
all over with the picador.   But now the chulos came to the
rescue.   Three or four flaunted their cloaks in his face and
drew his attention to themselves.   As he advanced, however,
these agile men slipped aside, and the bull struck only the

cloaks which passed lightly over his head. While this was being done, other men assisted the fallen picador to get upon his feet. He could not have risen without aid, for besides being bruised by his fall, his legs were encased in iron plates of great weight, made to resist the bull's horns. As for the poor horse, he was left to die in agony, writhing upon the sand, while his life-blood poured out in streams, as he struggled impotently to rise. By this time the bull had charged furiously upon the other picador. Almost the same scene was now repeated, save that the bull succeeded in plunging only one horn into the horse's side. Therefore, for the next five or ten minutes, this wretched animal actually galloped about the arena, urged hither and thither by his rider, while his entrails were dragging around his heels, and the blood was gushing forth in copious jets. I need hardly say that the ladies of our party shielded their eyes from this horrible sight. A German lady near me wept. But the fair Spaniards seemed to think of nothing but the men and the bull.

The second horse also soon dropped in the agonies of death, and, as new picadors came in, the bull, within fifteen minutes, had killed three horses outright and horribly wounded a fourth.

Presently he stopped as if exhausted. The practiced eye of the governor detected the moment for a change of tactics. He gave a signal, which was followed by a blast from the trumpet, and the picadors withdrew from the arena, much to our relief, although the weltering corpses of three horses still lay upon the sand. The chulos now came prominently forward to take a more decided part in the contest than they had previously assumed, and to perform some of their daring feats. One of them ran boldly out to meet the bull, as if he were to encounter a pet dog. My heart stood still a moment at the man's audacity. On came the bull, his blood-stained horns pointed directly at his daring foe.

"He is lost!" I said to myself, as the bull's head was lowered to receive him. But no; for planting his foot between
the horns, the chulo took a flying leap, and landed safely on
his feet, amid a tempest of applause, while the astonished
bull looked perfectly dumbfounded at his disappearance.
But this was nothing to what followed; for by the time the
bull had turned and caught
a glimpse of him, the chulo
had obtained a pole, with
which he coolly waited for

A LEAP OVER THE HORNS.

the charge. He had not long to wait. Of all the lively animals I ever saw, that bull would take the palm. Apparently
he did not pause to draw a breath, but darted forward with
the air of certain victory. It was indeed a hazardous act
that this bold chulo now performed, for he was forced to
calculate, at some distance, just when to jump, since if he
leaped too soon, the bull would have a chance to halt and
receive him on his uplifted horns. In any case the pole is
liable to be knocked from under him, and he must see to it
that he alights on his feet, or he will be speedily despatched.
Of course, no chulo would have dared to do this when the
bull was fresh; but now fatigue had rendered his charges

DEAD IN THE ARENA.

shorter and more easily avoided. What wonder that he was
wearied? Up to this time his exertions had been tremendous.
The perspiration glistened on his panting sides, and blood
coated both shoulders with a crimson mantle, proving that
the lances of the picadors had done their work.

After this sport had gone on for some time, the trumpets
sounded a new signal, and the banderilleros made their
appearance, to exhibit feats of even greater daring and
adroitness. One after another placed himself before the bull
and goaded him to madness by shaking in his face two colored
wands, on the extremities of which were twisted barbs.
When the angry animal made a dash at his tormentor, the
critical moment came. The banderillero waited until the
head of the charging beast was within his grasp, and then,
reaching between the advancing horns, thrust the colored
shafts into the shoulders of the bull! There was a horrible
fascination in this, for it was done just as the bull lowered
his head to toss his enemy to the sky. At one moment the
man seemed doomed to instant death. The next we saw him
leap lightly aside, while the baffled bull fairly bounded up
and down under the stab of the two darts, which remained

fixed in his bleeding neck. Another banderillero now took his position before the bull, and the same exciting scene again ensued, until, by a succession of such performances, the wearied and tormented animal bore many of these pointed shafts, which he in vain attempted to shake out of his flesh.

But one may ask, "What can induce men to adopt such a foolhardy business as this?" Partly, no doubt, the fame they thus acquire. Their names are household words in Spain, and they themselves are looked upon as demigods. Then, too, aside from their magnificent toilettes of silk and satin, glittering with gems, their salaries are enormous. The chief matador, whose duty it is on a Sunday afternoon to kill only two bulls, sometimes receives for this task about three thousand dollars. Frascuelo, "the first swordsman in Spain," demanded and received four thousand dollars for every appearance. The men below him were also paid in proportion to the risk they run; and as these toreadors are engaged for months ahead in the various amphi-theatres, it is easy to see that in Spain it is more profitable to kill bulls on Sunday than in America to preach sermons.

THE BULL HARASSED BY DOGS

But this was not all. When the banderilleros were exhausted, fierce dogs were let loose in the ring to rouse the wearied bull to a new pitch of fury. Just at the moment when one of these dogs had been tossed into the air, and I was all aquiver with excitement, I felt a gentle pressure on my shoulder. Turning my head, I saw a small, white hand, —a lady's hand—clutching unconsciously the lapel of my coat to steady herself as she leaned forward to obtain a better view of the arena.

"Oh, Harry," cried the owner of that little hand, "is n't it just splendid! Three dogs have got him now. He cannot shake them off!"

"Do n't you feel faint?" inquired her companion; "had n't you better go out now?"

"Oh, dear," was the reply; "I know it 's dreadful, but I 'm not a particle faint. On the contrary, I 'm so excited I could scream this minute."

"Well, you had better let go that gentleman's coat," he whispered with a laugh.

At last another flourish of trumpets gave the signal for the closing scene.

The matador entered the arena, and, being a special favorite with the public, was received with exultant cheers. With slow and dignified step this admired hero and pet of the ladies advanced to the royal box, and asked permission to kill the bull in a way that should do honor to all Spain. This being granted, he turned about and faced the bull. In one hand he carried a small red cloak, in the other a straight Toledo blade. All eyes were fixed upon him. Thousands of hearts were beating with excitement. The silence was impressive. The combat had reduced itself to a duel, with no hope of mercy even for the matador, for in that amphitheatre were fifteen thousand eager critics, from whom the slightest nervousness on his part would bring down jeers and cries, until the wretched man might lose his self-control and possibly his life.

Advancing to within a few feet of the bull, he irritated him a little with the cloak, and made a few passes in order to study his wiles. If it be a bold bull which he thus tries, there is little danger, for such a one usually shuts his eyes and madly rushes ahead; but the sly bulls, those which advance and then retreat, and seek to outwit their antagonists, require close attention. A skillful matador, however, can usually choose the place where he will lure the bull and

finally kill him; and if the matador's lady-love be in the amphitheatre, depend upon it, it is at the point nearest her that the bull will die.

A DYING MATADOR.

Frascuelo used to say that the matador's trade was a safe one, when well learned, provided the bull had never "performed" before, since experience renders them almost as wily as the bull-fighter; and it is a significant fact that the bull which recently killed Frascuelo had appeared in the arena at least once before. It is evident, therefore, that the most experienced matador sometimes fails. Accordingly, what courage, coolness, hope, and perhaps fear are concentrated in that moment! For in this deadly game he knows that one must die, and both may, since, though the chulos may leap the barrier, it would be dishonorable for the matador to try to escape. No matter what happens, he must stand his ground.

Nor can this trying moment be prolonged — the feelings of the populace will not bear suspense.   At length the bull made a grand rush forward.   This was what the matador desired. Instead of leaping aside, he planted his feet firmly, the mantle dropped as if by magic, and the Toledo blade, like a flash of lightning, entered between the shoulder and neck of the bull, and pierced the heart; and while the victor whirled to one side and bowed to the audience, the bull halted, staggered a few steps, and then, struck as it were with instantaneous paralysis, fell at his conqueror's feet,—his recent fury, life, and passion gone forever.

Thunders of applause greeted this dénouement of the tragedy, and the gorgeously dressed matador quitted the amphitheatre, bowing to right and left, and evidently feeling himself to be upon the pinnacle of glory.   In three minutes the bodies of the dead bull and horses had been removed by a train of mules with tinkling bells, and all was ready for a new combat.   For a bull-fight in Spain usually comprises six distinct tournaments such as I have described; and if the day be a particularly sacred one, seven bulls are slain to gratify the populace.   The sport is not, however, so monotonous as might be imagined, for the animals differ from each other in courage and ability.   We had the somewhat exceptional fortune to see, during the afternoon, one cowardly bull.   It was the second one that entered the arena.   Instead of charging directly on the chulos and picadors, this timid animal ran around the ring, seeking some way of escape.   Observing this, the picadors rode directly up to him and pricked him with their lances.   Even then the bull would not actually fight, but merely pretended to charge upon the horses, turning away at the last moment without giving the fatal thrust.   Then rose a perfect storm of yells, screams, and derisive shouts. So great was the noise that it was impossible to make ourselves heard by each other save by shouting.   Scores of oranges were hurled by the audience at the unlucky bull. "Put him out!" "Out with him!" was the verdict of the fifteen thousand spectators. This was soon seen to be a necessity, for neither chulos nor banderilleros could exasperate him to a charge. Accordingly, he was ignominiously rejected. A gate was opened, and six or eight tame steers were allowed to enter the arena. The coward immediately joined them, and they were all driven out together.

It is well known that, notwithstanding the skill of the participants, fatal accidents sometimes occur in these encounters, and frequently there are hair-breadth escapes. The famous matador Frascuelo was once about to give a bull the *coup de grace*, when the cunning animal, by a peculiar jerk of the head, twisted the sword

PLAYING AT "TORO."

from the matador's hand. Disdaining to run, the matador stood his ground. On came the bull, and catching the man upon one horn, held him there for five minutes, and ran with him around and around the ring despite all the efforts of the chulos to release him. At last he flung him into the air. The horrified spectators expected, of course, to see him fall a mangled corpse. Instead of that, the matador arose and assured the audience that the bull had not harmed him in the least. The horn had slipped between his girdle and his shirt!

"Did he afterwards kill the bull?" I asked.

"Oh, señor," was the reply, "I never saw a bull killed

so beautifully. You see, Frascuelo was so angry that he thrust his sword in to the very hilt, and held it there till hand and arm were crimsoned.''

Another marvelous escape from death was told me by Patricio. A banderillero, in running from a bull, was just

CORDOVA.

about to leap the barrier, when he fell. He rose and tried to leap again, but the infuriated bull was close upon him. Instinctively the man drew himself up into the smallest possible space and pressed his body tightly against the barrier. A second more, and the bull's horns had passed, one on each side of him, and stuck fast in the wooden fence, leaving about an inch of space between the man's waist and the monster's head.

"Did that man ever have nerve enough to fight again?'' I asked.

"Of course,'' was the reply; "it was he who thrust the darts so splendidly to-day.''

Perhaps the most remarkable fact connected with Spanish bull-fighting is the fascination that it has for children. Their

favorite sport is to imitate its horrors. The boys all play at
"Toro," as they call it, indoors in winter, out of doors in
summer, enacting every scene of the arena, and carefully observing every rule which there prevails. Thus, trained to it
from infancy, we cannot wonder that, as men, they see no
harm in such amusements, and even arrange special bull-
fights to assist the church, or help some charity, or even to
raise funds for the Society for the Prevention of Cruelty to
Animals.

From Madrid, a railway journey of a few hours brought
us to Cordova,—a place so thronged with interesting memo-
rials that it is difficult to know which one to study first.
Every part of Cordova, to him who hears aright, is eloquent
of ancient grandeur. More than two thousand years ago it
was a famous city. The river that still glides by its walls
had then been darkened by the shadows of Rome's legions, and

even the bridge
that echoes to
our horse's feet
to-day rests on
foundations laid
by order of a
Roman emper-
or when Christ
was still a child
in Galilee.

AN ANCIENT GATE, CORDOVA.

But the es-
pecial glory of
Cordova dates
from its conquest by the Moors. With their advent so brilliant
an era of prosperity was ushered in that it received the name
of the "Athens of the West." Indeed, the description of the
wealth, luxury, and refinement of Cordova under the Moors

reads like an Eastern tale. In the tenth century, when most of Christian Europe was sunk in the depths of ignorance, witchcraft, and semi-barbarism, Cordova possessed nearly a million inhabitants. Within its walls then were six hundred mosques, fifty hospitals, nine hundred baths, six hundred inns, eight hundred schools, and a library of six hundred thousand volumes, although, four centuries later, the royal library of France consisted of only nine hundred volumes.

ENTRANCE TO THE MOSQUE OF CORDOVA.

"The Arabs," says the great scientist and philosopher, Humboldt, "deserve to be regarded as the veritable founders of physical science, even taking those words in the extended sense which they bear to-day. They may almost be said to have created botany. Chemistry is no less indebted to them. They cultivated geography and geometry with success. Astronomy especially owes to them an extensive development, and they determined the

duration of the earth's annual revolution with an exactness
which differs but one or two minutes from the most recent
calculations."

One relic of the Moors in Cordova is the ruined tower
of Abd-er-Rahman—the most enlightened of all the Moorish
caliphs. Once
it formed part
of his magnifi-
cent palace,
but now, in its

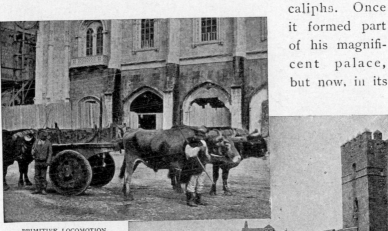

PRIMITIVE LOCOMOTION.

THE ROMAN BRIDGE, CORDOVA.

mournful isola-
tion, it merely
serves as a re-
minder of that
glorious era,
when by the
order of this
Abd-er-Rahman, the streets of Cordova were the first paved in
Europe,—admirably constructed two hundred years before
the first paving-stone was laid in Paris.   Then one could
walk at night for miles in Cordova, illumined all the way by
public lamps, seven hundred years before the first street
lamp was lit in London; and Moors were writing scientific
treatises and encyclopædias in Cordova when many Christian
princes could scarcely sign their names.   It was a terrible day
for Spain when these high-bred, artistic Moors were driven

out of this country which they had ruled so well for centuries. Wealth, learning, art, industry, and the charm of Oriental life, to a great extent, went with them, and Spain has been lower in the scale of prosperity and intelligence ever since.

Nowhere did I realize this more effectually than when I looked upon a typical Cordovan wagon, with its clumsy frame, and wheels of ill-shaped, solid blocks of wood. Yet this primitive style of locomotion is characteristic of large sections of Spain. To a system of agriculture which, under the Arabs, made of this country the garden of the world, has succeeded a method which uses the root of a tree for a plough, and for the means of transportation the back of a donkey or a wretched vehicle worthy of China. Since the expulsion of the Moors the population of Cordova has dwindled from a million to forty thousand. Its nine hundred public baths have disappeared; its six hundred inns have been reduced to four; its skill and industry have vanished; the light of its great universities has been put out; and, to crown all, in one of the provinces of Andalusia, the country of the gifted Moors, in whose embrace are Cordova, Seville, and Granada, out of a population of three hundred and sixty thousand, but a few years ago, more than three hundred thousand could not read or write.

THE ORANGE-GROVE BEFORE THE MOSQUE.

Nevertheless, one marvelous monument remains in Cordova to attest its ancient glory. It is the Moorish mosque,

—unique and without a rival in the world. This alone would repay a special visit to Spain. It is true, the exterior of the building reveals at present nothing either Moorish or beautiful; for it has suffered shameful desecration. When the Christians captured the city, they dedicated this structure to the Virgin Mary, and sought to "purify" it by defacing its Mohammedan decorations. Be-

THE GATE OF PARDON (CLOSED).

(OPEN.)

fore this mosque, for example, in the time of the Moors, was (and, for that matter, still is) a beautiful courtyard filled with orange-trees, and forming a kind of vestibule to the mosque itself. Standing here beneath the snowy orange-blossoms, the Moslem saw before him then a façade of nineteen beautiful horseshoe arches, separated from each other by magnificent columns, and open continually between the orange-grove on one side and the grand interior on the other. Now, however, these pillars are badly mutilated, and all the arches are walled up, save one.

Leading into this courtyard from the street is a pretty portal known as the "Gate of Pardon." I gently pushed this

open, and felt as if a picture of the Orient had suddenly been placed before me, set in a sculptured frame. How charming was the scene disclosed through this old Moorish gateway! In the distance was the court-

IN THE MOSQUE OF CORDOVA.

yard of the mosque, containing cypresses and cedars, orange-trees three centuries old, and palm-trees of unknown antiquity. A wave of perfume rolled out toward us through the open door, like that which greets one when he enters a conservatory; and eagerly crossing the court we stood within the mosque itself. Anticipate what you will, no disappointment here is possible. I halted spellbound at the threshold. Before me stretched away in shadowy perspective a marble plain surpassing in extent the mighty area of St. Peter's,— six hundred and forty feet in length, four hundred and sixty feet in breadth—and from this rose in perfect regularity one thousand and ninety-six resplendent columns. It is, in truth, a sculptured forest, each tree of which is a single shaft of jasper, porphyry, or pure alabaster. We knew not where to turn, bewildered by the intricacy of these glittering avenues,—

nineteen in one direction, twenty-nine in the other, crossing
each other at right angles, and forming endless paths of softened light and shade.   What stories of the past these columns
seem to whisper to us, as we pass between them!   This may
have come from the site of Carthage, and on its polished form
the hand of Cæsar or of Scipio may have rested; these were
a gift from the proud caliph of Damascus; that one was
brought from ruined Ephesus, and may have pleased the eye
of Cleopatra or St. Paul; and these are from Jerusalem, and
on them Jesus may have looked.   Truly, therefore, in the
dusky aisles of this marble forest are memories which make
the heart beat quickly and the eyes grow dim.   Everywhere we fancy we can see reflected from these polished shafts

(as in a line
of magic mir-
rors) the stately
pageants of the
past, and in
these corridors
we seem to
hear, commin-
gled with our
footfalls, the
muffled echoes
of antiquity.

A fragment
of the old Moor-
ish ceiling was
recently discov-
ered here.   The

A SCULPTURED FOREST.

wood is arbor vitæ, which is considered practically incor-
ruptible — at all events, this portion is as sound to-day as
when placed here eleven hundred years ago.   Yet how feebly
do these relics represent the former splendor of this structure!

Then, suspended from the ceiling, carved to represent over-hanging tropical foliage, four thousand seven hundred gilded lamps lit up with rainbow colors twelve hundred of these

columns, and made the rich mosaics in the walls seem like a sacred tapestry of gold. The floors, too, were covered with Oriental rugs, and in the shadow of these polished shafts knelt hundreds of adoring wor-shipers. But acting through

A SECTION OF THE CEILING IN THE MOSQUE OF CORDOVA.

misguided bigotry, the Spaniards whitewashed and destroyed the sculptured ceiling of cedar-wood, so beautiful as to be worthy of the Alhambra. All the outside aisles were filled with tawdry chapels, thus walling in more than one hundred splendid monoliths; and sixty more columns were leveled in the centre of the mosque to make room for an ugly chapel two hundred feet in length, which, in this maze of slender columns, looks like a hideous tumor, obstructs the view, and exasperates the beholder.

When Charles V, who was himself something of a vandal, beheld this act of barbarism, he was indignant with the monks who had effected it, exclaiming, "You have built here what might have been built anywhere, but you have destroyed what was unique in the world." It was then, however, too late for repentance: the irreparable evil had been done.

Some years ago, the Emperor of Morocco visited Cordova; and as he knelt and prayed within this sanctuary of his ancestors, while the Spanish priests were chanting vespers in the chapel, he bowed his head and wept, feeling himself an outcast and stranger in this magnificent memorial of that Moorish genius, which, alas! has passed away forever!

From Cordova, a railroad journey of five hours brought us to Seville. "Sevilla!" shouted an enthusiastic Spaniard, as our train drew near it, and leaning out of the car window,

SEVILLE.

gazed long and lovingly upon this city which he called his home. No wonder he was proud of it, for clasping it in beauty, like a silver girdle, was the stately river whose

Moorish name, even when pronounced in English,—the
Guadalquivir,—sounds like a strain of music; while in the
distance rose above all other objects that graceful Moorish
tower known as the Gi-
ralda.

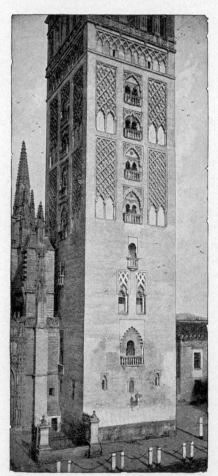

SECTION OF THE GIRALDA.

As we drew nearer to
the city, this tower grew
still more distinct and
prominent, rising beside
the vast cathedral which
was once a Moorish
mosque. The Giralda
was then the minaret of
the Moslem sanctuary, and
from its sculptured gal-
leries came the muezzin's
call to prayer, just as it
does from all the minarets
of the East to-day. All
famous cities have some
magnet of attraction,
which stands distinctively
associated with their
names; and, as Rome
possesses her St. Peter's,
Naples her lava-crowned
Vesuvius, Athens her
Acropolis, and Pisa her
leaning tower,—so Seville
boasts of her Giralda!

Under the Moors this must have been wonderfully beautiful. It
rises to the height of three hundred and fifty feet, and its
square walls were originally decorated with elegant designs on
a background of rose-color, fragments of which still remain

At that time its summit was surmounted with four enormous golden balls, whose lustre was discernible at a distance of twenty-five miles, and whose value was no less than two hundred and fifty thousand dollars. But these costly ornaments were destroyed by an earthquake in 1395, and now the Giralda is crowned by a colossal female figure in bronze, which, although fourteen feet in height, and weighing more than a ton, is nevertheless so nicely balanced, that it turns with the slightest breeze. Oddly enough, this statue represents Faith. Truly, a strange subject for a weather-vane, never steadfast, but blown about by every wind. I suspect the architect was a practical joker.

This spire soon faded from our view amid the bustle and excitement of arrival, as we drove rapidly through the streets to our hotel. How thoroughly Spanish were the sights around us! Now we were passing by a crowded market-place, where sunburnt peasants offered fruit for sale in a wild medley of discordant cries, —their wares meantime protected by rude awnings, antique enough to pass for Roman togas rescued from the rag-bag, but rivaling in hues young Joseph's coat of many colors. The awnings were, however, quite essential both for men and fruit.

It was with pleasure that I reached at last the shady court of my hotel. How grateful and

THE GIRALDA.

V. — 21

refreshing after the hot ride was its cool garden! I felt as if I had entered an oasis, and understood at once the Moslem's love for shade and fountains and the great part they play in stories of the Arabian Nights.

Seville is the Paris of Andalusia, the gayest city of all Spain, the home of Figaro and Don Juan. Glittering like a jewel on the banks of the Guadalquivir, environed by orange-groves and palms, and glowing under an ardent sun, it is

almost an Oriental city. Its inhabitants are the merriest of all Spaniards, and, like the Neapolitans, are careless children of the sun. Many of them seem to live — who can tell how? — on an orange or a bit of bread, yet they always have strength

A SPANISH MARKET-PLACE.

enough left to thrum a guitar or dance a fandango. They sleep on the steps of churches, they warm themselves in the sun, and know of heaven only what they see of it through the smoke of their cigarettes.

I shall not soon forget my first siesta in Seville. Seated beneath a canopy of vines, I listened to the murmur of a neighboring fountain, above which rose at times the throbbing tones of a guitar. Just opposite, upon a balcony, I saw a Spanish lady toying with her fan. Somewhere the tremulous tones of silver-throated bells were calling men to prayer. Here was, in truth, a combination of impressions, which left no doubt that I was actually in Spain.

At length, refreshed by an hour of repose, we started out to view Seville in the cool of the afternoon. A few steps brought us to

THE CATHEDRAL AT SEVILLE.

an open rectangle which bears the appropriate name of the "New Square." New, indeed it is. The Moor of seven

IN SPANISH GARDENS.

centuries ago would smile disdainfully at such an imitation of northern towns, and pointing to his narrow streets, in which the sun can only fully enter for an hour at noon, would ask if his were not a system better suited to the climate. For it is no trifling matter to cross this stretch of fiery sunlight in the summer heat. Some slender palm-trees, it is true, raise here and there their feathery screens against the overpowering sun, but these are not sufficient. If, therefore, in the early afternoon this square appears deserted, it is because the long siesta is not yet concluded, during which time, the Spaniards say, no one stirs out in the sun save dogs and Englishmen. But could we enter at that hour one of the private houses of Seville, we should find luxuries enough to warrant this desertion of the public squares. Nothing

A SPANISH COURTYARD.

can be more charming than the appearance of these open courtyards, even from the street. We look in through a trellised gate, and see almost invariably a pretty *patio* with marble pavement, enclosed by walls enameled with bright tiles. Sometimes an awning is stretched over it; oftener a grapevine forms a thick roof with its broad, green leaves. At all events, no matter how plain the exterior of a Spanish house may be, it always has its open court, adorned with flowers, orange-trees, and possibly a fountain, where, in the evening, may be heard the sound of a piano or guitar, or the melody of a song. But when one turns to behold the exterior of some of the houses, he frequently concludes that life here after all is not so attractive. The windows are covered with heavy iron bars, as if the build-ings were safe-deposit vaults instead of pri-vate houses. These gratings, while intended to protect the family plate, are also meant to guard the young ladies of the household. But, as the song

GRATED WINDOWS.

assures us, "Love will find the way;" and so, no matter how narrow the opening in a Spanish balcony may be, it is never too small for the tiny hand of an Andalusian lady. Hence, on our evening walks, we often saw beneath one of these cruel lat-tices a lover armed with a guitar, and hold-ing within his hand a small, white object glistening in the moonlight, which he from time to time would press fer-vently to his lips.

A RELIGIOUS PROCESSION IN SEVILLE.

One day, in strolling through the streets of Seville, we saw approaching us a religious procession, conveying through the city paintings and holy relics of the church.

PALACE OF SAN TELMO.

Times change indeed, and we change with them. Eighteen hundred years ago Venus was worshiped in Seville, and at that time her statue was borne through the streets as that of the Virgin Mary is to-day. In fact, quite early in the Christian era, during a festival of Venus in Seville, two maidens, who had been recently converted to Christianity, refused to render homage to the goddess, and were put to death. These martyred girls became the patron saints of Seville, and, so far as protecting real estate is concerned, very successful ones they seem to have been. For tradition says that, in 1504, during a terrific thunder-storm, the devil tried to blow the Giralda over. To overturn a tower three hundred and fifty feet in height is no easy undertaking, even for the devil; yet it is claimed that Satan would have done it but for those pretty patronesses. They wound their white arms tightly round the tower, and clung to it so firmly that it did not move. Do not regard this as an unimportant story. It is portrayed on canvas or in sculpture in almost every sanctuary of Seville, and even Murillo consecrated to this breezy legend one of his finest paintings. I once heard a heretic remark that, if those saints were really as beautiful as Murillo represented them, he wished he could have changed places with the Giralda during that heavy gale.

On our first evening in Seville, we made our way to its most fashionable promenade, bordered on one side by the handsome palace of San Telmo, the home of the Duke of Montpensier. This avenue is deserted by day, but after sunset is usually thronged with joyous people. It was, I recollect, one of those perfect nights which form the charm of southern Spain. The sun, the tyrant of the day, had disappeared. Its burning heat had been succeeded by delicious coolness; and now, refreshed by their siestas, yet with a trace of the sun's fire tingling in their veins, the gay Sevillians seemed to have taken a new lease of life. The costumes of the men were, as a rule, such as one may find in any part of Europe. Among the ladies, we did not see a single hat or bonnet. Such innovations may be tolerated in Madrid, but the Sevillians

A SEÑORITA.

draw about their handsome tresses lace mantillas, which, when coquettishly adorned with a red or pink rose, are

THE TOWER OF GOLD.

certainly the prettiest and most becoming head-dresses in the world. More-over, with an art peculiar to themselves, these fair Sevillians open and close incessantly their restless fans,—each motion, it is said, conveying a meaning to the initiated. Court-ship by this means, there-fore, has become a science, for, in addition to such gestures, these Spanish belles send forth from their dark eyes glances which can be best described as a startling combination of velvet and fire. As for the peril of flirtation with them, the traveler may well recall the sad ex-perience of one who sings —

"One evening when the setting sun
Was gleaming on the Guadalquivir,
To gold converting, one by one,
The ripples of that mighty river;
Beside me on the bank was seated
A Seville girl with jet-black hair,
And eyes that might the world have cheated,
A wild, bright, wicked, diamond pair!

"She stooped and wrote upon the sand
(Just as the brilliant sun was going)
With such a small, white, shining hand,
I could have sworn 't was silver flowing!
Her words were three, and not one more; —
What think you could the sentence be?

The siren wrote upon the shore:
  ' Death, not inconstancy.'

"And then her two large liquid eyes
    So looked in mine, that (devil take me!)
I set the world on fire with sighs,
    And was the fool she chose to make me!
St. Francis might have been deceived
    By such an eye and such a hand,
But one week later I believed
    As much the woman as the sand!"

In one of the streets of this attractive city we were shown
a little wine-shop, said to have been the home of the "Barber

SPANISH BEGGARS.

of Seville," whom the novel of Beaumarchais and the Opera
of Rossini have made immortal. Unfortunately, however, no
sooner had our carriage halted before it than we were

surrounded by several of those beggars who are, in southern Spain especially, an intolerable nuisance. The Spaniards, in their grandiloquent form of speaking, have for these mendicants a particular formula, which is supposed to banish them as rapidly as Persian insect-powder does the pests of Spanish inns. They bravely address them with the words *"Perdone usted, por Dios, hermano!"* [For God's sake, excuse me, brother!]. Guide-books recommend this phrase, and I tried it several times, but with no effect. When, therefore, my

IN THE GROUNDS OF SAN TELMO.

patience was exhausted, I usually fell back on the shorter and much more pointed remark of *"Al demonio!"* which at least relieved my feelings, for it means in plain English, "Go to the devil!"

Upon the bank of the Guadalquivir stands a conspicuous feature of Seville, known as the Tower of Gold. Originally a Moorish structure of defense, it was used by the Spaniards as the treasure-house, in which, amid the blare of trumpets and the enthusiastic shouts of the exultant populace, were stored the enormous quantities of gold brought by Columbus and other brave discoverers from the New World, and fondly deemed by Spain exhaustless. No doubt the memory of this brilliant tower lingered in the minds of Pizarro, Cortez, and Columbus long

after their departure from Seville, and it formed as well the goal
of their ambition when, after years of toil and conquest, they
once more ascended the Guadalquivir with their precious spoils.

AN ARCH IN THE ALCÁZAR OF SEVILLE.

The gardens of San Telmo, as well as those of the Alcázar
of Seville, are beautiful. Renewing the system of irrigation
which the Moors brought to such perfection, the Spaniards

have introduced into these parks the waters of the Guadalquivir and made of them a partial vision of the Orient.
Here, as in several localities in southern Spain, we noted with
especial pleasure the beautiful symbol of the East,—the tree

of romance and
poetry—the
palm. Spain
owes this also
to the Moors;
for the first
palm-tree ever
seen in Spain
was planted at
Cordova by
Abd-er-Rah-
man, who de-
sired to have
here a memorial
of his much-
loved Damas-

IN THE ALCÁZAR, SEVILLE.

cus. Truly, it is not strange that the palm-tree has been
worshiped by the children of the sun; for it not only shelters
them from the ardent heat, but gives to them, unasked, the
most nutritious fruit, and, surviving through many generations, like a beneficent deity, waves over them its rustling
boughs as if in constant benediction.

One of the most precious monuments of Moorish art in
Spain is the Alcázar of Seville. When the Christians had
driven the Moors from this city, the conquering monarchs
took up their residence here; but when they wished to embel-
lish and enlarge the palace they were too wise to employ
their own architects for such a work, and accordingly, during
a time of peace, sent to Granada for Moorish aid. How
beautiful are the results of their labor! For one who has

not seen the Alhambra, it is difficult to imagine anything
more exquisite than this Alcázar of Seville.   For, thanks to
the skill and talent of these Moorish workmen, another Alad-
din-like palace here sprang into existence, almost rivaling the
Alhambra.   Here, as there, one fancies himself in some
enchanted palace, whose carved and colored walls resemble a
continuous network of gold and lace.   The arches in the
courtyard, resting on marble columns, are beautifully carved
and perforated, and glitter with gilding and brilliant colors.
The doors, too, are of cedar-wood inlaid with pearl, and
around the walls we see a continuous expanse of the unrivaled Moorish tiles.   Moreover, unlike much of the Alhambra, which has fallen into ruin this exquisite work has been
so carefully restored that it now gleams with almost the same

brilliancy and
beauty as when
it echoed to
the footsteps of
the Moors.

This charm-
ing palace pos-
sesses for every
visitor from the
New World a
special interest;
for it was here
that Queen Isa-
bella gave her
private jewels
to Columbus,

COURTYARD OF THE ALCÁZAR, SEVILLE.

that he might have the means requisite for his voyage of
discovery.   In imagination, therefore, we can almost see the
brave-hearted discoverer, his face kindled with the glow of
hope regained after years of sad delay, kneeling before that

gracious sovereign, whose wise courage and judicious patron-
age will ever remain a glorious honor to her memory. A
casket of jewels does not seem much in itself, yet it sufficed
in this case to change the destinies of two worlds.

But all the souvenirs of this Alcázar are by no means so
attractive. Around it cluster also gloomy memories which
seem to have no fitness for so fair a spot; for these mosaic
pavements have been reddened by the blood of murdered
relatives and guests, and the atrocious deeds of Don Pedro,
whom history has branded with the title of "The Cruel," have

cast a lurid light
upon these rich-
ly decorated
halls. It was,
for example,
through these
apartments
that, sword in
hand, this Nero
of Seville, pur-
sued his broth-
er, whom he
hated with jeal-

GARDENS OF THE ALCÁZAR, SEVILLE.

ous fury; and here the unhappy victim was at last struck
down by the blows of the courtiers; while Don Pedro,
coming up to where his brother lay quivering on the pavement, looked at him attentively, and then drawing his
dagger, handed it to an African slave to give the wounded
man his death-blow. This done, he calmly re-entered the
palace and sat down with invited guests to dinner.

The most delightful portion of a tour in Spain is that
devoted to Granada and the Alhambra. In the southeastern
part of the Spanish peninsula lies an enchanting plain some

THE ALHAMBRA AND GRANADA.

thirty miles in length, green as the richest moss, partly
enclosed by picturesque hills and dominated by the snow-
crowned Sierra Nevada.   This beautiful expanse of verdure
is dotted with innumerable white-walled villages and towers,
as a rare Oriental rug might be adorned with pearls.   At one
extremity of this valley, which has often been the scene of
desperate conflicts between Moors and Christians, two famous

objects glitter
in the sun,—
one on the plain
itself, the other
seated like a
queen upon a
lofty throne:
the first is the
city of Granada,
the second the
palatial fortress
of the Moors,—
the world-re-
nowned Alham-
bra.   Granada,
—which by the
way is the birth-

THE ALHAMBRA AND PLAIN OF GRANADA.

place of Eugénie, the ex-Empress of France,— is said to
have derived its name from the granates or pomegranates,
which flourished here seven centuries ago as they do to-day.
It is still one of the largest cities of Spain, although its population is but seventy-five thousand, as contrasted with four
hundred thousand in the time of the Moors.

Above the town itself rises a steep hill, not unlike the
Acropolis of Athens, crowned with the favorite home of the
Moorish caliphs.   The name Alhambra appropriately signifies
"Red Castle;" for its walls and towers, emerging from an

V.— 22

ocean of green foliage at their base, glow with a beautiful vermilion tint, in striking contrast to the blackness with which the hand of Time too frequently enshrouds the ancient edifices of the North.

The ascent to the Alhambra is easy. Broad avenues, often completely embowered in the shade of giant elms, one

ON THE ALHAMBRA HILL.

hundred feet in height, lead the way upward in gradual curves over finely graded terraces. There are certain glorious sensations in the life of every enthusiastic traveler, which in a moment repay him for weeks of absence, privation, and fatigue. No amount of travel can take anything from the thrill of emotion with which one first beholds certain historic sites. Such a spot is the Alhambra, — a gem dimmed and flawed by the rude grasp of many conquerors, but still so marvelously beautiful as to draw to itself admirers from every quarter of the globe. As I

ONE OF THE VERMILION TOWERS.

rode up this steep ascent and rapidly approached its storied courts, I felt as I did when gliding into Venice, or entering imperial Rome, or when my gaze first rested on the gilded domes of Moscow, or my feet trod the rough pavement of Jerusalem. Nor is the charm here purely one of history; for over these terraces stream numerous cascades, in channels framed with ivy leaves and verdant moss. In fact,

LOOSED FROM THE MOUNTAIN FASTNESSES ABOVE.

the music of fountains or cascades, loosed from the moun
tain fastnesses above, greets one at every turn. We found the
air here in the month of May as soft as in Greece or Egypt.
Nightingales were singing in the abundant foliage, while the
delicious perfume of orange-flowers and roses, which lined
the walls at frequent intervals, made breathing a luxury and
mere existence a delight.

Approaching finally the terminus of these curving avenues, we stood
before a large
square tower of
imposing aspect.
It is the entrance
to the Granadan
Acropolis, and
bears the title
of the Gate of
Justice, because
the Moorish
sovereign for-
merly sat here
to dispense jus-
tice to his sub-
jects,—a custom

THE TOWER OF JUSTICE.

always common in the East, and one repeatedly mentioned
in the Hebrew Scriptures. An inscription over the doorway
reads: "May the Almighty make this portal a protecting
bulwark, and write down its erection among the imperishable
actions of the just!"

Beneath the arch is an altar dedicated to the Virgin; and
it was before this that the first mass was said after the conquest of Granada, while the Moors, with tear-dimmed eyes,
were traversing the mountains on their way to Africa. This
tower, like all the rest of the Alhambra battlements, is severely

THE GATE OF JUSTICE.

plain, but such external plainness is characteristic of most Eastern architecture. The Orientals superstitiously avoid

the evil eye of envy, and rarely show the world the treasures they possess. So it was here. Externally the Alhambra was a frowning fortress; internally it was a voluptuous palace. Without, one looked on unattractive walls; within, one

THE ALHAMBRA'S BELT OF MASONRY.

found the most enchanting ornamentation that the world has seen. The Alhambra resembles, therefore, a valiant warrior,—fierce and unyielding in the heat of battle, yet full of tenderness in hours of relaxation.

PALACE OF CHARLES V AND THE ALHAMBRA.

Passing beyond this Gate of Justice we found ourselves in
an extensive area, like the courtyard of a castle. "Where is
the Alhambra?" I asked in disappointment; for I had expected to step at once into its famous halls. Instead of that,
before us rose, from a mass of shrubbery and flowers, the
ruined palace of Charles V,—begun but never finished by that

THE PALACE OF CHARLES V.

emperor, who had resolved to build here something better than
the Alhambra. Accordingly, in obedience to that royal whim,
a large part of the Moorish palace was torn down to make room
for this structure, which seems as much out of place within
these walls as did the Christian chapel in the Mosque of
Cordova.

The interior of the ruined palace of Charles V is a place
where travelers sometimes feel a trifle nervous in the evening.

In fact, during my stay on the Alhambra Hill, a great excitement was caused one morning by the declaration of a French gentleman that he had been dogged by footpads here the night before.   He said he had been forced at last to run from them, arriving pale and breathless at the hotel door.   Inves-

ORNAMENTATION OF THE ALHAMBRA.

tigation proved, however, that the reputed footpads were agents of the Government, ordered to keep close watch on relic-hunters, and they had deemed the Frenchman's fear a proof of guilt.

Leaving this useless ruin, we eagerly passed through a modest doorway and stood in the Alhambra itself.   At once,

INTERIOR OF THE PALACE OF CHARLES V.

as though by a magician's spell, we seemed to have passed from Europe into Asia. We were in the Court of Myrtles. The blue dome of the sky was above us, and beneath were marble slabs, whose spotless whiteness was once surpassed by the snowy feet of the fair sultanas who lightly trod them, for this was the bathing-place of the wives of the caliphs.

In the centre is still a marble basin of water, one hundred and thirty feet in length, now tenanted by goldfish and surrounded by hedges of myrtle and orange-trees, bright with their glistening leaves and golden fruit. At each end of this enclosure we saw a row of slender marble columns

MURAL ALCOVE, ALHAMBRA.

supporting walls which looked like chiseled ivory. Above us was a characteristic Alhambra roof, composed of countless bits of cedar-wood inlaid with mother-of-pearl, and looking like the cells of a honeycomb or a grotto of stalactites. The whole place seemed so delicate and dainty, that I at first had scruples about walking freely on its marble pavement. In the walls are little openings surmounted by exquisitely sculptured arches, resembling the convolutions of a shell. It is supposed

A COURT IN THE ALHAMBRA.

by some that these tiny mural alcoves held the slippers of the sultanas while they went to bathe. Others maintain that they contained some of the rare Alhambra vases; while others still believe that here were placed at night elegant porcelain lamps to shed a softened light upon the matchless decorations of the walls. However this may be, it is impossible to linger in this lovely court without imagining scenes which must have once occurred beneath these delicate arcades, when a sultana made her toilette attended by her female slaves. It seems incredible that this fair palace has not been tenanted for centuries. Everything here seems merely awaiting the return of some princess of the Arabian Nights.

"Do you hear that song of the nightingale outside the walls?" asked my guide, Mariano, as I stood here. "In those notes, we fancy we hear the voices of the lost sultanas, who return thus in spirit to haunt their earthly paradise."

From the Court of Myrtles it is but a step to the Hall of Ambassadors,—the grand reception-room of the Moorish sovereigns. How is it possible to describe this apartment, in which, nevertheless, we lingered hour after hour during those bright May days? Piercing the thick Alhambra walls are nine elaborate windows, whose exquisitely chiseled arches seem as unsubstantial as frost-work; while so glorious is

ARABIC INSCRIPTIONS AND STUCCOED TAPESTRY.

the view which they command, that at one of them Charles V is said to have exclaimed, sighing in pity for the exiled Moor, "Unhappy the man who lost all this!" Between these windows, and around the walls to the height of three or four feet, is a continuous expanse of the unrivaled Moorish tiles; and above these the mural decorations are so beautiful, that as I beheld them outlined against the azure of the Spanish sky, seen through the casements, I could think of nothing but a

gorgeous mantle of finely woven, cream-colored lace, suspended near a robe of light blue silk; for, indeed, all the
designs of the celebrated Spanish lace sold at Granada are
copied from the walls of the Alhambra.   It was here especially that Washington
Irving loved to read
and write; and the swal-
lows which he described
as twittering about the
historic hall still dart
in and out through the
marble arches, and rest
upon the cedar-wood
lattices in the high wall,
through which, doubt-
less, many a fair sul-
tana has often gazed,
unobserved, on the fes-
tivities below.

ENTRANCE TO MOSQUE, IN THE ALHAMBRA.

To comprehend bet-
ter the beauty of the
walls of the Alhambra, we must remember that they were
formerly colored and gilded, as is evident from the traces of
such ornamentation that remain.   Truly, they must have
then resembled silken nets of gold embroidery, containing
countless intricate designs.   It is interesting to note how the
religious faith of these Moslems affected the architecture of their
dwellings; for all this stucco tapestry has, interwoven with its
gossamer fretwork, a multitude of Arabic inscriptions, ming-
ling in frostlike tracery with the leaves and flowers, and
meaning "Blessing," "Welcome," "God is our Refuge,"
"Praise be to God," and, above all, the motto, "There is no
conqueror but God," words which the Moorish chieftain uttered
to his subjects when they came forth to meet him returning

victorious to Granada. Accordingly, these walls, many of which were destroyed by the priests as being pagan, are really poems proclaiming the goodness and greatness of God and forever wedded to the silent music of architecture.

Bearing these facts in mind, we entered the charming Mosque of the Alhambra, intended as a place of worship for the inmates of the palace. This was an essential part of such a structure; for the Moors were a profoundly religious race, as all Mohammedans are to-day. Emerging from the Orient,—that cradle of the world's religions,—it was their wonderful religious zeal which enabled them to overrun the borders of the Mediterranean, wresting from Christian hands the cities of the Cross. Nor has their fervor vanished yet.

THE MOSQUE OF THE ALHAMBRA.

No portion of the human race is so invariably devout as are Mohammedan believers. No matter where he is or in what he is engaged, five times a day, on the arrival of the hours for prayer, the Moslem will excuse himself and kneel in reverence—if not within a mosque, then on the deck of a steamer or on the desert sand—without a particle of ostentation, or, on the other hand, of shame, at thus confessing the preëminence of God.

What an ideal life of luxury and beauty this Moorish palace, even in its ruin, brings before us! Here, when the town below lay panting in the tropic heat, within this cool and silent palace, finished like a jewel, and glittering with all the colors of the Orient, the Moorish monarchs and their friends would pass the hours of summer enjoying the cool air from the adjacent mountains, and lulled by the murmur of numerous fountains into that dreamy languor so loved by all inhabitants of the East. For every room in the Alhambra had its marble fountain; and almost every corridor its rivulet of crystal water, connecting one fountain with another and filling the air with freshness and the perpetual cadence of a song.

THE ALHAMBRA TOWERS.

It is said, too, that the Moorish ladies, whose beauty lent to this incomparable edifice an added charm, were finely formed, graceful in their manners, and fascinating in their conversation. The Arab poets say of them that when they smiled they displayed teeth of dazzling whiteness, while their breath was like the perfume of flowers. Yet it was not altogether a life of idle pleasure that was here maintained.

The Moorish sovereigns were valiant warriors, and some were
noted for their love of intellectual pursuits. Thus, King Al-
hamar, founder of this palace, was an illustrious proof of
what these cultivated Moors could be and do. His was an
age of poetry, art, and music. The language spoken at his
court was the most elegant Arabic. He founded schools and
hospitals; he offered premiums to the best artisans; fostered
the manufacture of silk, until the tissues of Granada surpassed even those of Syria in beauty; and, best of all, he
began this splendid palace, inspiring all the workmen, as
they labored, with his own enthusiasm.

Standing at one of the windows here, one looks across a
deep ravine, upon a hill
directly opposite

THE WINE GATE OF THE ALHAMBRA.

the Alhambra.   It is thickly covered with trees and shrubs, among which are innumerable caverns cut in the solid rock. These are the homes of the famous Spanish gypsies, chiefly found in Andalusia.   It would seem that the sun of southern Spain, which has an almost Oriental splendor, allures these gypsies hither from their native land; for undoubtedly they are of Eastern origin.   Until within a few years, they have been unruly members of society, setting at defiance both laws and police; but now they are held to a strict account for their deeds and are also liable for military service. On approaching one of their hillside caverns, a gypsy woman will bring forth to

THE COURT OF THE LIONS.

you from a squalid room a cup of coffee, for which you must pay liberally or else be exposed to great annoyance.   The men among these gypsies are for the most part horse-traders and blacksmiths; the women make their fortunes by pretending to tell those of others and by selling fancy articles; and I hardly need add that men, women, and children are experts in the art of thieving.

v. — 23

The masterpiece of the Alhambra is the "Court of the Lions." It occupies the centre of the palace and is surrounded by a spacious courtyard, once paved with blocks of snow-white marble, fragments of which remain. Around it on each side are galleries and pavilions, which, in their elegance and lightness, are the despair of architects and the admiration of the world. They are supported by no less than one hundred and twenty-four marble columns, apparently too slender and delicate to bear even the fairy-like arches that rest upon them. The Alhambra looks as though it had risen from the earth, like a palace of fairies, at the mere wave of an enchanter's wand. In reality it required one hundred years to ripen slowly to perfection. The amount of labor expended on it was enormous. Some one has well suggested that it is possible to find in this style of architecture a trace of the former wandering habits of the Moors. In exchanging their nomadic for a settled life in Spain, did they not imitate in their architecture the luxurious shawls and hangings of their former dwellings,— erecting, instead of a tent-pole, a slender marble column and covering their walls with colors and gilding in place of the silken tissues of Damascus?

Yet, if the tourist anticipates grand proportions and massive Gothic pillars in the Alhambra he will be disappointed. Moorish art has its own distinctive character and conditions, within which it is unrivaled. Moreover, it should be always borne in mind that the Alhambra was a southern palace, whose architecture, unlike the Gothic forest of the north, resembles rather an Oriental flower, glowing with all the vivid colors and redolent with the sweet perfumes of Asia.

In the centre of the Court of the Lions stands its crowning beauty, like a precious stone mounted in a most brilliant setting. It is an alabaster fountain, the spray from which once fell almost within the galleries themselves. The basin of this fountain is one solid piece of alabaster, ten and a half

THE SUMMER PALACE OF THE MOORS, GRANADA.

feet thick, and rests upon twelve strangely sculptured lions, which give to the court its name. Around its edge is an Arabic inscription, on which the eyes of many a Moorish caliph and sultana must have often rested. A portion of it reads as follows: "Look at this solid mass of pearl spreading through the air its prismatic shower! One might imagine it to be a block of glistening ice, with crystal water melting from it." Its concluding words doubtless express the unuttered prayer of every visitor to the Alhambra: "The

COLUMNS OF ALABASTER.

blessing of God be with thee evermore; may thy pleasures be multiplied, and thine enemies destroyed."

"But how is it possible," every tourist asks at first, "that the Moors, whose architecture is replete with elegance and grace, could have ever sculptured such strange-looking animals as these and called them lions?" It is easily explained. The Koran expressly forbids any representation of animal life, lest it should lead the Moslems to idolatry,—thus cutting them off at once from both painting and sculpture, in which perhaps the Arabs would have excelled as wonderfully as in architecture.

It really seems, however, as if these beasts could be safely worshiped without violating one of the old Hebrew Commandments, at least; for they resemble nothing either in heaven above or the earth beneath, or in the waters under the earth.

It was by moonlight in this lovely court that I took my

THE ALHAMBRA BATTLEMENTS.

farewell look at this gem of Moorish art and Oriental beauty. The rays of the crescent moon (the glorious symbol of Islam), striking these slender pillars obliquely, gave to them the transparency of alabaster, yet clothed them with a dust of gold. Through the perforated carvings of the galleries, the moonbeams darted in like silver arrows, as if to pierce the once richly gilded capitals of the marble shafts. As I gazed,

I felt as if I were removed from the world of reality, and were wandering in a moonlit palace of alabaster in the time of the Arabian Nights. Lingering here, I asked myself, how could a brave and cultivated race like this have been so utterly destroyed and driven out of Spain, where they had ruled for a period almost as long as that which has elapsed since the conquest of England by William the Conqueror? To solve this mystery, I rose and passed beneath a graceful arch into a room

A STREET IN GRANADA.

which, although exquisitely decorated, is haunted with appalling memories. It is the Hall of the Abencerrages,— named thus in honor of the bravest and most brilliant family that ever graced the court of the Alhambra. Yet at this fountain, it is said, thirty-six princes of that clan were treacherously murdered,—beheaded, one by one, as they were admitted to an audience with their jealous sovereign. Deeds like this can best explain to us the mystery of the Moorish downfall. It is the old, old story of internal weakness and dissension. For where the caliph's wives were numerous, each one aspired to have her son succeed his father on the throne, and wished that the sons of other consorts should be considered illegitimate. And thus arose within these halls those plots and intrigues, which form the usual history of Oriental dynasties and pave the way to crime and ruin. Hence, when the Moors had become enervated by luxury and intrigue, their fate was sealed. A less refined but sturdier race was to supplant them, and did so in the very year that it also went forth to find and conquer a New World.

Upon the second day of January, 1492, the plain before Granada was covered with a Spanish army, impatient to advance and take possession of the Moorish palace. For the long and memorable war had ended with the surrender of Granada. It was a perfect morning. The old vermilion towers of the Alhambra gleamed beneath a cloudless sky. Among the Moors a melancholy silence prevailed, but on the

A BIT OF THE ALHAMBRA WALLS.

plain below the air was rent with shouts of victory and hymns of praise. The Spanish army was drawn up in line, their banners fluttering, their swords and armor glittering in the sun. Meanwhile, from a humble gate beneath the Tower of Justice, a mournful cavalcade came sorrowfully forth. It was composed of the family of Boabdil, last of the sovereigns of Granada, and had been thus sent off privately in advance, that they might not behold the exultation, possibly the insults, of the enemy. They were to proceed to a lonely spot and wait there until he should overtake them. His mother, it is said, rode on in

THE ALHAMBRA HILL.

silence, pale as death, yet able to control her feelings; but his young wife gave way to bitter lamentation, and had to be supported by her faithful guards, who walked beside her horse, themselves quite overcome with grief.

Meantime, from another part of the Alhambra walls emerged Boabdil, with some fifty cavaliers, and rode sadly downward toward the plain. In his hand he

AMONG THE MOORS IN AFRICA.

held the keys of the Alhambra, and as he approached King Ferdinand he gave them to his conqueror, exclaiming: "These keys are thine, O King, since Allah has decreed it." Then with the melancholy of a broken heart, he made this one request, that the gate through which he had just come to yield his palace and his kingdom should be walled up, never again to be repassed by mortal foot. The Spaniard granted his entreaty; and, in fact, the portal was closed up with masonry and has remained so ever since.

One of the mountains near Granada is still called "The Last Sigh of the Moor," because upon its crest the retreating monarch gazed for the last time on the Alhambra. This last Moorish gem had been transferred to the Spanish crown, the banner of the Christians floated over the vermilion towers, and all was lost. Behind him lay the most exquisite situation on earth; before him lay the desert of

Africa, as cheerless as the prospects of a dethroned fugitive. What wonder that he wept in anguish, exclaiming: "God is great, but when did ever misfortune equal mine?" Yet his mother embittered his grief by exclaiming, "You weep now like a woman over what you could not defend as a man."

> "The fascination and allure
> Of the sweet landscape chain our will;
> We also linger on the hill,
> Our parted lips are breathing still
> The last sigh of the Moor."

Beyond the summit where Boabdil breathed farewell to his ancestral home rises the chain of the Sierra Nevada, covered

HE IS THINKING OF GRANADA.

with dazzling snow, and piercing the blue sky at a height of eleven thousand feet. Rightly did the Arab poets compare these mountains to a sparkling mass of mother-of-pearl,—a vision never to be forgotten. They have been the pride of Granada ever since fleet horsemen used to bring ice in baskets from their sparkling heights, to cool the drink of the Moorish kings. Beautiful in form and color, they stand above this Damascus of the West like beneficent deities, fanning her with cooling breezes, tempering her summer heat, and feeding her limpid rivers from an unfailing treasure-house of snow. What a contrast between this earthly paradise and the present home of the Moors in Africa! Their glory is departed. Little remains to them now save bitter memories. With the exception of the Jews, there is not another such case as theirs in history. Spain still appears to them as a "Paradise Lost." There is a sadness in the face of every genuine Moor that I have ever seen. Reserved and melancholy, with features rarely brightened by a smile, they seem to bear the consciousness of a lost paradise. It is said that some of them even now re-

ROCK OF GIBRALTAR.

tain the keys to their old family homes in Spain. And to this day, when one of their number is unusually pensive or sad, his comrades will whisper as they point to him, " He is thinking of Granada."

The last portion of Spain to linger in my vision as I left its shores was the Rock of Gibraltar, crouched like a monster sphinx upon the border of the sea, guarding the most important gateway of the world. Although bristling with English cannon and surmounted by the British flag, this mountain is still an eloquent memorial of the Arabs; for Gibraltar is only a corruption of Gebel-al-Tarik,—the mountain of Tarik, the leader of the Moors when they first landed in Spain. What wonder that the ancients called this the Pillar of Hercules, planted by the gods at the western extremity of the universe, beyond which even the boldest never dared to sail? As I beheld this gateway of the west, upon whose base the waves of two great oceans break in ceaseless cadence,

I realized, with a pang of regret, that the fascinating book of Spanish travel was closing fast; and as the mists of evening veiled it gradually from my view, I murmured: "Farewell, vermilion towers of Granada! Farewell, embroidered walls of the Alhambra; sweet orange-groves of Andalusia; fair Giralda of Seville; and marble forests of the Mosque of Cordova! It is a joy forever to have seen you. Hereafter in the picture-gallery of my memory there will hang no more brilliant and alluring tableaux than those which are tinted by the sun of Spain."

Aus Kemper 10/24/1947